Digging Deeper into God's Truth Defines a "Christian"

MALARA HAS ALSO WRITTEN:

1. The Bible on How to Box

2. Celebrity Sculptures & Hands of Stone, My Story

3. God's Clarity Through Poetry

4. God's Clarity Through Poetry 2

5. **Digging Deeper into God's Truth Defines a Christian**

6. The Guide to Christian Dating, Marriage, and Sex

7. IT'S ALL SUBJECT TO GOD'S WORD

8. Examine The End Times

9. Many Beliefs, But God

For each publication I authored, I created a short video explaining it. These books are available online or on my website. Please take a look.

www.josephmalara.com

Contents edited by Aimee Malara

Cover design by Aimee Malara

Written by Joseph Malara

DIGGING DEEPER INTO GOD'S TRUTH DEFINES A "CHRISTIAN"
Copyright © 2020, Joseph Malara **Revised Copyright © 2026
Joseph Malara**

ISBN: 978-0-578-63401-2

I have revised and updated this book, along with others, to ensure they remain current, clearer, and more comprehensive, offering better explanations and information for all readers. Each book is available worldwide online and can be viewed or purchased on my website. I also created a short video for each book I authored, explaining its contents. Please visit www.JosephMalara.com

I pray that God uses even these humble books He has allowed me to write to draw YOU closer to HIM.

Email me for more information or questions you may have, JosephMalara@yahoo.com

To order additional copies (e-book, audiobook, or paperback) and to view all other books and their videos, please visit: www.JosephMalara.com

Contents

Digging Deeper into God's Truth Defines a "Christian"
(*Written by Theologian*, Joseph Malara)

Forewords

Foreword: Pastor Jim McClarty

There are libraries full of books about Christianity that support every known theological position. They present a widely varied and utterly bewildering spectrum, ranging from intense hermeneutics to little more than fantasy and wild imagination. But the confusion is easily swept aside by following a simple biblical mandate: Preach the word (2Tim. 4:2).

The word of God is the standard for all Christian thought, doctrine, and practice. The Bible is its own best authority. Every opinion, speculation, or commentary on the Bible must be compared to the clarity and authority of the Bible itself. Those are not mere platitudes. They are the expected standards of Christian authorship.

Yet, it's that very standard that seems most lacking in the vast majority of books concerning Christianity. The lack of a clear, concise biblical presentation is what leaves most "Christian" books wanting. The Bible says tough things. Some of what it declares is hard to wrap our minds around. Sub-biblical thoughts of men and women are more comfortable to wear and easier on our pride. But the Bible says what it says. And it either means what it says, or it doesn't.

That's what Joseph Malara's book is about. Rather than shying away from the sometimes-difficult truths of Scripture, Mr. Malara meets them head-on. If you're looking for a pop-psychology book to help you raise better children through sports analogies and fishing stories, this book is not for you. But if you've ever wrestled with some of the tough stuff in the Bible and you're looking for clarity, you've come to the right place.

Maybe you're just wondering about Jonah's preaching, or you're confused about tithing. Is God all-loving, or what about getting involved in politics? Those are some of the questions Mr. Malara addresses and answers with his hand firmly on the text of Holy Writ.

Personally, I wish more books were similarly grounded in God's word. The tough stuff is worth wrestling with. Yet, as often as not, it's avoided. As one of my professors used to tell me, "The cure for wrong use is NO use. The cure for wrong use is right use."

This, then, is a book for people looking for the proper use. The approach to Digging Deeper Into God's Truth defines a "Christian" as starting and ending with the word of God.

Read this book with your Bible in hand, prayer on your lips, and a willingness to stand toe-to-toe with God's word and let it say what it says. Then, apply accordingly.

Jim McClarty
Pastor: Grace Christian Assembly, Smyrna, TN

Foreword Chaplain, Ed Alvarez

I think it is quite admirable and a significant undertaking to write over 100 pages, when most Christians can't even write 100 words about our Blessed Lord. This book is an easy and insightful read and is right on point with what is going on today concerning modern day evangelicalism. A MUST READ!

Ed Alvarez
Chaplain, Inspire Bible Fellowship
Tamarac Fl.

Foreword: Pastor, Scott Ryan

Joseph Malara wants the Church to go deep – deeper into the Word! Our God is a God whose depths are unsearchable and the way we get to know God more is through His Word. I love how Joseph desires to point the Church to Scripture itself - if we want to know God, we cannot fashion God into something that comes out of our own imagination. What Joseph makes explicitly clear in this book is that your ideas about God must come directly from what He's revealed about Himself - and where do we find His Self-Revelation? Go to Scripture! Read! Study! Go deep! And, of course apply to your life!

This book is a special call to the Church to take God at His Word - to conform our lives to who God has revealed Himself to be. Furthermore, this is not merely an ivory tower-type of treatise – Joseph is someone who's lived this. What hits home with the reader is that God's truth saved Joseph, molded him, and I was particularly moved by Joseph's testimony, his belief in thinking that he was "saved" a long time ago yet through the Lord's conviction he came to realize that he wasn't truly saved. Once God quickened Joseph, he began plumbing the depths of the Bible and learning from more mature brothers what true, saving knowledge of the Lord is. It's his own story that resonates and it's also the story of every Believer who has fallen under the conviction of God Himself, that we are all completely lost in our sins and only Christ alone can save.

I am grateful for Malara's passionate plea to the Church to get serious about God and His Word and living it out in society. Joseph is calling us to "take up and study," to stop the "happy meal-type" of Christian life – stop feeding yourself with spiritual milk or worse, spiritual artificial sweetener. Stop attending "churches" that sugarcoat everything but are not teaching the Bible. If God is God and everything we do is based on Him, wouldn't we want to know Him? Again, Joseph is speaking to the Church – he is looking at the Church on the inside and offering a special plea – go deeper with God!

Scott Ryan
Pastor: Chinese Baptist Church of Coral Springs, Fl.

Acknowledgements

I want to thank God my Father for giving me His Son, Jesus, and Jesus for giving me the Holy Spirit. I love You, my God and my Lord! Thank You for Your Holy Word and for bringing me to my knees and opening my ears and eyes to You.

My prayers were answered when You brought my precious Aimee, my beautiful wife, into my heart and my life. You have proven to me that prayer is powerful, and You alone open doors and place the right people in our lives.

I want to thank Aimee for her unwavering support and assistance in correcting my countless errors and in arranging time for me to write. I am in awe of her patience with me; her smile at the dawn of each day and her kiss at the close of each night; she has brought new radiant sunshine, inspiration, and purpose into my life, which we both will use to glorify God. This book would not have been started or completed without her in my life and God in my heart. Aimee brings me joy and genuine laughter each day. She is much more than I prayed for and more than I have even dreamed of. She prays with and for me each day. We study God's Word together daily, and she wants to; she is a Proverbs 31 woman. God, I owe everything to You! Thank You Jesus!

Introduction

I want to write here a brief breakdown or correlation for the reader, whether they are in Christ or not. If you read this book, I ask that you please read it through to its end, and don't be offended by the truths, meanings, and words you will read. It's a window into God's Truths, because I use the Bible to interpret the Bible.

God's Word will hopefully be more apparent to the reader after this book. Remember this, as you read this book, **I am writing to Believers**. If, while reading this book, you disagree with any areas or chapters, that's fine; please e-mail me, and I will try to get to all e-mails in due time. If you are not saved when you read this book, remember this: I was 19 and swore I was "saved, born again." I was misinformed and absolutely wrong in my total assessment of Salvation and its direct cause-and-effect on and in my life.

Although I was not saved at 19, but saved for real at 48, it was God's Will to "Save" me, not mine. So, if you are not saved and this book reveals that, or exposes it, please don't despair; the fact that you are even reading this book proves one thing: you are searching. You may be 19 or 99 years old; God may open both your eyes to His Truths today or tomorrow, only God knows when or if. I know one thing for sure; it's *Jeremiah ESV 29:13 You will seek me and find me, when you seek me with all your heart.* Here lies the conundrum... this book aims to unpack this mystery in a way we all may grasp.

Can one truly seek God with all their heart without His help? Let's begin to dig, Philippians NKJV 1:6 says *being confident of this very thing, that He who has begun a good*

9

work in you will complete it until the day of Jesus Christ; If God is moving or planning to do "a good work" in you, let His Scripture used in this book bless you, edify you, mature you, and may He use it in such a way, only He can. Today could be the day God chooses to do a good work in you, and or to soften and open your heart entirely to Him. So, please pick up your Bible and use it to confirm my writings, as if your life depended on it, because it does... let's dig in! Use a highlighter and/or pen and underline pertinent areas, even in this mere book.

Throughout this book, I will refer to this paragraph as (point #1). Please keep that in mind; it means it's never too late. Allow God to be God and work in your heart. Salvation and sanctification may be a breath away...

Luke 24:45 NIV: *Then he (Jesus) opened their minds so they could understand the Scriptures.* I pray the same to you the reader, even to open your mind to this simple book... As I continue to write, regardless of the name you have, or the title on earth you achieved, may God bless your reading of this book and use it to enrich, enlighten, and encourage your seeking, your new walk, or your continued walk with Jesus the Christ.

Here is a poem I wrote that I will include in each book God allows me to write moving forward. It's true and still sends chills up and down my spine...

Poem Summary

The poem you are about to read is an accurate account of my Christian conversion. I was not even thinking about salvation. I was alone in pain, crying out in self-pity to a God I thought I knew. When you read this poem, you will see how God opened my closed eyes, softened my hard heart, transformed my weak mind, and converted my lost soul, awakening me from spiritual death to spiritual life in Him; it happened in the blink of an eye. He has given me a thirst for His Word and His Truths. The morning after that life-changing night went like this...

The next morning, I reached out to a "Christian" friend by phone, the very moment I awoke, while still sitting at my bedside. The first question I asked him was, *"How do you study the Bible?"* He asked me if I had a Bible Concordance; my reply to him was, *"Whatever that is, I will meet you in 45 minutes at the bookstore to get one..."* The rest is History...

God, I thought I knew

On my knees, desperately broken, crying out loud, out loud to a God I thought I knew, but didn't...

I cried hard, "Take my life, I have done nothing good with it." ...nothing seemed to fit...

I cried and cried endless tears falling down my face, for my family gone, my shame, my guilt, my sin, knowing nothing would be the same, my life totally misplaced, but unbeknownst to me, there was much more I could not see...that would soon, soon take place...

I cried out, "Take my life, I have done nothing good with it," as my tears fell like heavy rain. I moaned and suffered with each grieving tear drop, greater and greater pain...

Alone in my anguish, sobbing uncontrollably, crying out loud to a God I thought I knew, but didn't...Unbeknownst to me...

I thought I was reaching out for God to hear me...but He was reaching down to me to be heard...

He said, **"Read The Bible...Read My Word."**

I clearly unmistakably heard...with my ears, my heart or a spiritual part? In the body or out...only God knows...

As chills rolled up and down my spine...was this all in my mind? No...I was in awe, and today I am still in it...a total surprise...as my tears immediately stopped flowing from my eyes...my heart skipped a beat, my eyes widened...Who did I just meet?

I became quiet and still; it was clear to see...His Peace overcame me...

I was spiritually dead, until He said, what He said...

That night I went to sleep with calm, I never ever knew...woke with a Biblical thirst, so miraculously anew...

He Called me...Now I do clearly perceive what I could never ever on my own...know, desire, or hunger to believe ...

His plan for me that night, to un-blind me and give me His clear sight...up to then, I lived recklessly through my foolish self-induced misery...crying out to a God I thought I knew...but didn't...Pretending to be a true believer but all the while, a self-deceiver...a make-believer...

I am now all His, and His Good News I do tell...His Mercy Saved me from myself...and from an eternal Hell...

Although that night, I begged Him to take, take my life...and, He did...

He took my old life and gave me New Life in Him...and took away my sin...I am now Born Again...through Grace by Him.

This is my testimony, so true...the night I cried out...cried out to a God, I thought I knew...

Luke 18:13 LSB

But the tax collector, standing some distance away, was even unwilling to lift up his eyes to heaven, but was beating his chest, saying, 'God, be merciful to me, the sinner!'

Chapter 1: What is Election and What is Born Again?

I find this topic of great importance when I travel to visit "churches" and when I speak to those who attend a "church" of some sort. I discovered that so few, if any, truly know, understand, or care to know God's doctrine of Election. This reflects the sad and inaccurate state of those who collectively avoid the whole teaching of God's Word. This exposes the "user-friendly churches", the "entertainment churches", and the "dead churches" and who they honestly are and who they truly represent, **the misinformed and the lost.**

Teaching around the topic of Election, or avoiding it altogether, is what I see throughout 90% of "Christian" type "churches." To do so, one therefore dances around God's Truths as if some truths are more important than others. Churches do this because they crave money, ratings, mega-sized buildings, **and large congregations of the lost**, as if that's God's purpose, when the opposite is true. God wants to get His Truths out to His People, so they can grow in His Truths, sharing and teaching others as His Word teaches us; this Spiritual growth process is called sanctification. But if you and those you listen to are in error, how would you know whom you should listen to; wouldn't you also be guilty of false teaching? Is your Pastor correct? This is why I was moved to write this book. Let's look at Matthew 28:18-20 NIV: *Then Jesus came to them and said, "All authority in heaven and on earth has been given to me. Therefore, go and make disciples of all nations, baptizing them in the name of the Father and of the Son and of the Holy Spirit, and teaching them to obey everything I have commanded you. And surely I am with you always, to the very end of the age."* This is known as **The Great Commission**; here, Jesus leaves no doubt of His Deity. He Commands all His Followers to make Disciples and to Teach. All true Believers are to teach others God's Truths; it's a Command.

Most of today's "pastors" are not "born again" themselves. You ask, "How can that be so?" God still honors His Truths, regardless of who speaks them. This brings me to explore and examine this so critical topic. When I was about 15 years old, I started delivering milk as a helper, door to door, back then in bottles! While the milk man's name was Charlie, he was a Christian, the first Believer I met. Charlie witnessed to me countless times, telling me about the Gospel and explaining Jesus. But being a Catholic, I felt I was good, so his efforts didn't move me. When I was 19, I was invited to attend a church where my best friend went, so I went. After the service, I walked that aisle, had a big smile, prayed "that prayer," and, weeks later, got baptized. Then, a few weeks later, I went "soul winning," which meant going from house to house with my then "pastor," telling others about the Gospel. I was in "church" two or three times a week for years! I even had bumper stickers on my car professing Jesus!

Why am I even bringing this all up? Because I lived the next 28 years thinking I was truly saved, when I was far, far, far from it. I was as lost as lost could be; yet I told others I was a "believer." I thought I had some form of fire insurance (from Hell), some security, or good standing, like God and I were good, a feeling of acceptance from God because I said yes to Him; yet I lived for only me. And all that was a lie; I was living a lie. This is where most so-called "believers" are today. Remember this, there are three (3) types of believers: "Believers", "Un-believers", and "Make Believers"; I was a Make Believer, yet I didn't even realize that at the time. This is the damage today's so-called "pastors" create. It's a "false belief," a "false jesus" and a "false hope." That was the *"God I thought I knew"*, that was the Poem I included in this book, and it will also be in all the books God allows me to write. My first poetry book included poems that weren't entirely biblically accurate. As a new Christian, I asked my old friend Charlie to read it and confirm that the poems aligned with God's Word; he even wrote the foreword. However, after reading the entire Bible, I found many biblical concepts that were inaccurate, which led me to write "God's Clarity Through Poetry 2" to correct those errors. It excites me to know that God can use even poems to open closed eyes! Let's look at Ephesians 1:4-6 KJV *"According as he hath chosen us in him before the foundation of the world, that we should be holy and without blame before him in love: Having predestinated us unto the adoption of children by Jesus Christ to himself according to the good pleasure of his will."*

The Apostle Paul wrote Ephesians, addressed to Believers (it's essential to know a writer's audience). Again, Paul is writing to Believers, not unbelievers. Let's unpack this verse. It says He Chose Us, God Chose Us, but when did He? Before He created this world, He adopted Us (Elect) in Christ according to HIS WILL; many skim right over these words as if they don't exist. Then it says, according to God's Good Pleasure, He chose us. We did not choose Him. It was ALL His Will, not ours. The confidence of Salvation rests exclusively in the Authority of God, for God is the guarantee that ALL He has Chosen will without fail come to Him for Salvation.

Look over to John 1:12-13 KJV *But to as many as received him to them gave he power to become the sons of God, even to them that believe on his name, which were born not of blood, nor of the will of the flesh, **nor of the will of man, but*** *of God.* Therefore, one can only receive Him once God opens one's eyes and ears to Him and His Gospel. God's Word makes it very clear there is no free will to choose God; it is ONLY His Will (GOD'S WILL) to choose His Children, and **children never get to choose their parents.** It's not a natural thing but a "supernatural" thing that God is solely in charge of every one of His Chosen, each person He Elected. He will not share His Glory with anyone; no one can say they are more intelligent or wiser to choose Jesus, because no one, truly on their own merit, or of their own will, chose Him or did choose Him. It's not what are you going to do with the Lord Jesus? He is the Lord; it's what is He going to do with you? Let's look at Ephesians 2:8-9 KJV *For by grace are ye saved through <u>faith</u>; and that <u>not</u> of yourselves: it is the <u>gift of God</u>: Not of works, lest any man should boast.* Paul, addressing Believers, is saying no one can earn their salvation (trying to do so is useless); it is ALL by God's doing, His Grace. If it were based on anything someone did, it would not be **Grace.** Let's not confuse this verse or any verse in the Bible. **Works truly save Christians, the Works of Jesus!** It's ALL about Jesus; the whole Bible is a Love Letter from God about Jesus.

This passage of scripture also says it's a Gift of God, and gifts are not earned nor can you claim or choose a gift, so here we see that even <u>Faith</u> is God's <u>Gift</u> to His Children. God's Salvation depends on neither our merit, nor our will, and despite our disobedience, despite our arrogance, despite our wickedness, such will not nullify His Elective purpose. **God is Faithful even though His Children are not.** If it were not for God's Sovereign Will, His Mercy, His Grace, there would be no one going to Heaven, not one! John MacArthur, a Reformed Baptist Pastor and Teacher concerning Bible Verses, once said, *"What does this verse mean to you? That* *isn't the question. What would this verse mean if you never existed? It doesn't matter what it means to you. It means what God intended it to mean.*" End of quote, so **Digging Deeper into God's Truth Defines a Christian.**

Let's continue to dig in. Let's define the word "Gift" as "A thing given willingly to someone without payment." This would exclude those who think they can ask for a gift. Gifts, in and of themselves, are not asked for; thus, the word "gift." Try stopping someone in the street and saying, *"Where's my gift?"* Let me know how that works out for you. Here's a little story that will help explain Mercy and Grace. A Police officer pulls over a car that was speeding on the highway. Before the officer can say anything, the driver says, *"I know I was speeding."* The officer says to the driver, *"You deserve a speeding ticket, but I am going to let you off with only a warning."* That's Mercy! You see, the officer is within his rights to issue that driver a speeding ticket by law. Yet this officer chooses to show and extend Mercy to that driver. Mercy is an act of unmerited, undeserved forgiveness showing genuine compassion. **Mercy is NOT getting the punishment you deserve.** Now, the officer does one better, he says to the driver, I will NOT give you a ticket, that's Mercy, but then adds, *"I will give you a free voucher for 100 dollars to use at your favorite restaurant,"* That's Grace. **Grace is receiving a blessing you do NOT deserve**. Let's look at this now Biblically. Mercy is saving you from a burning, everlasting Hell. That in itself would be too much already, seeing by God's Word (as we shall soon see) we ALL deserve Hell. But God goes one better. He not only shows His Mercy by saving His Children from an eternity in Hell, but He also gives His Children eternity with Him in Heaven! Here, Grace is giving us "Heaven," which again none of us could ever, ever deserve.

Jump over to Ephesians 2:1 KJV *And you hath he quickened, who were dead in trespasses and sins;* Ephesians 2:4-5 KJV *But God who is rich in Mercy, for his great love wherewith he loved us. Even when we were dead in sins, hath quickened us together with Christ by grace ye are Saved.* Let's unpack these last two verses; you were dead, dead to Him, dead to Heaven. Dead in your own sins on your way to pay for them yourself in Hell, but God, rich in His Love, made Some Alive, Alive to Him, Alive for Heaven, Alive from the dead. Next time you walk past a cemetery, try yelling to the dead, see if any rise. They are dead; they can't rise, nor hear. This is the unbeliever's condition before <u>God quickened some</u>; those some are now Alive, to Him, to Heaven, to His Word, and removed from their sinful condition. **Those Few now have a sincere Thirst, a True Hunger for God's Word, His Truths, His Love; they crave to know Him and all about Him.** They want to repent of their sin, and they sincerely believe the Gospel with open eyes, hearts, and ears as never before!

The day before a person is "Saved," such a desire was not present in that person; there was no desire for such, no real want for doing what's right in God's eyes; by God's standards, not our own standards or this fallen world's standards or desires, but God's. Repentance is a turning from sin and a result of a changed life, **including a new hatred of sin that comes when God** quickens (gives life to) a heart for Him. This is the Power of God at work in His child's life.

When a person is saved, **EVERYTHING** changes, everything. You will think differently, your family and friends will all notice the "Christ-like" changes, and soon they will grow to hate you like Jesus was hated. It's Matthew 10:22 KJV: *And ye shall be hated of all men for my name's sake: but* *he that endureth to the end shall be saved.* Here, Jesus makes it very clear, but to make this even more straightforward, it's Matthew KJV 10:34-38 *Think not that I am come to send peace on earth: I came not to send peace, but a sword. For I am come to set a man at variance against his father, and the daughter against her mother, and the daughter in law against her mother in law. **And a man's foes shall be they of his own household.** He that loveth father or mother more than me is not worthy of me: and he that loveth son or daughter more than me is not worthy of me. And he that taketh not his cross, and followeth after me, is not worthy of me.* Here, Jesus explains that He came to divide, to open the eyes of His Elect, and this is evident in the reactions of those closest to you. **There will be division, not unity, not peace, division.** Once your eyes are open to God's Truths and you realize He has changed you, you crave to read His Word, you really want to talk about Him, and you want to witness to others, because you now have a burden for their lost souls. You will study His Word, and soon you will be able to identify the false "pastors" and "teachers" and not be moved by "candy-coated" false gospels. And you won't be moved or swayed if you hurt someone's "feelings." **It's not about feelings; it's about TRUTH. The Devil wants you to pay attention to your feelings; Jesus wants you to pay attention to His Truth.** You will grow to hate what God hates and love what God loves. **You will love Jesus because of Who He Is.** He alone is worthy of all your praise. The day before you were saved, all that was not present and was meaningless. You will try to tell others of your experience, but it will move very few. Remember this: no one is ever, ever responsible for another's Salvation, that responsibility is all God's.

Yes, we must always plant seeds of Truth and tell others about the Gospel because it is a divine command and important for salvation. This responsibility belongs to all Christians, not some. We should have a sincere desire to reach the Lost, the unsaved, driven by the Holy Spirit's prompting. Charles Haddon Spurgeon, known as "The Prince of Pastors," emphasized this when he said, *"If God would have painted a yellow stripe on the backs of the **Elect**, I would go around lifting shirts. But since he didn't, I must preach 'whosoever will' and when whosoever believes, I know he is one of the Elect."*

The Elect have a New Condition, a New Heart, a Re-Birth, thus the words "Born Again"; it is not a mere "religion," all other religions are manmade, Jesus called the religious people of His day hypocrites, therefore Christianity is truly exclusive. It's a life changed by God. Here, I must explain that there are two events in a Christian's life (Believer's Life) that are entirely under God's Control: the day the child is born and the day the child is Born Again, a 2nd Birth. A child never gets to choose; a child is helpless. Does a newborn baby decide to be born? No, he or she had undeniably, unquestionably nothing, nothing at all to do with their own conception; it was out of his or her ability. This analogy accurately reflects and supports the idea that being "Born Again" by God is a similar situation. **Life begins at conception; nothing grows if it's not living.** Once a child is conceived, life begins; once a person is "Born Again," a Re-Birth begins. Let's go to John 3:3 ESV *Jesus answered him, "Truly, truly, I say to you, unless one is born again he cannot see the kingdom of God."* Here we read Jesus telling a Jewish ruler named Nicodemus, a Pharisee of the Sanhedrin, that **being Born Again was the only way to see Heaven**. Some receive God's Mercy; others receive God's Justice; no one gets injustice. We all deserve HELL. Jesus didn't die on the cross merely to make Salvation possible. He died to redeem, purchase, and secure a people that He had set His love upon from **before the foundation of the world.**

Jump now to John 3:6-8 KJV: *that which is born of flesh is flesh; and that which is born of Spirit is spirit. Marvel not that I said unto thee ye must be born again. The wind bloweth where it wishes, and thou hearest the sound thereof, but canst not tell whence it cometh and whither it goeth: so is every one that is born of the Spirit.* Jesus is professing here that **it is supernatural and there is no human way to be "Born Again."** And no outward obvious appearance would determine such, and man does not control it, like the wind is not under our control. When Jesus speaks to unbelievers and believers alike, He must keep things simple. **He is God, and we are merely creatures from the dirt.**

John Calvin, the French theologian, back in 1519, having dug much deeper into the Word of God than most, revealed many truths. Let's use the mnemonic device used to explain the acronym T.U.L.I.P. to describe God's Election further. **The "T" stands for Total Depravity**, meaning humans by nature are thoroughly corrupt as a result of this fallen world due to Adam eating the forbidden fruit in the Garden of Eden. Let's look at Romans 3:10-12 KJV *As it is written, There is none righteous, **no not one.** There is none that understandeth, there is **none that seeketh after God.** They have all gone out of the way, they are together become unprofitable, there is none that doeth good, NO NOT ONE.* Here, Paul is making it very, very clear that **not one person is good, not even one**; he is quoting several Old Testament passages. **Not one person seeks God.** This is interesting, and once you realize how much God hates sin and what His Standards truly are, no one can seek Him with an honest heart. Many try, and what occurs is they find a "false god", a "religion", a **"false jesus",** worship an "idol", or create "their

22

own god" out of thin air, or "become their own god", notice the small **"g"**. **If you believe the wrong gospel, it does NOT matter how sincere you are in your belief; you are sincerely wrong.**

Let's jump over to Jeremiah 17:9 KJV *The heart is deceitful above all things, and desperately wicked: who can know it?* Here, the Prophet Jeremiah states that the actual condition of all our hearts is wicked. This is the heart of the un-saved man, the unregenerate heart, the false convert, the lost, those of the world. But for God, and His Mercy, His **Grace in the transforming of a heart from stone to Flesh; changing the condition of a heart from being of the world to being in The World and NOT of it**; changing hearts of stone into converted hearts of Flesh, ones after God's Own Heart, such a Heart is one of a Born-Again Believer.

Look now at Ephesians 2:3 KJV *....in times past the lusts of our flesh, fulfilling the desires of the flesh and the mind: and were by nature the children of wrath, even as others.* Remember here, Paul is writing to Believers, not unbelievers; saying before being Born Again, all people were children of wrath, meaning God's Wrath **(first death is physical, second meaning spiritual),** which translates to eternity in Hell to the lost or unbeliever. The flesh means self-effort, those things we can accomplish in our own strength, or intelligence, apart from God, since it is clear that man is utterly lost and incapable of choosing God and worshiping Him. God knows this and predestined some, His Elect, because of His Mercy and His Grace, which is completely undeserved and unmerited, and all God's Will, no one else's. **No one earns or deserves Grace, thus the word Grace.** Again, no child or unborn infant chooses their own parents. That's why God's Children are ALL adopted by God Himself. **If you think or somehow believe that you chose Jesus,**

you are very much mistaken. You may have been obedient in your response to His Call, but you cannot, nor would you do anything other than be overjoyed and totally elated by Him! You had NO choice; you could not have done anything other than come if CALLED by Almighty God. Oh, what a joy! **The fact that you had nothing to do with your own Salvation overjoys the Believer.** But leaves the "baby Christian," unbeliever, or "fake Christian" at odds with God's Truths, God's Sovereignty, let's continue to dig...

Let's go to Romans 8:14-15 KJV *For as many as are led by the Spirit of God, they are the sons of God. For ye have not received the spirit of bondage again to fear; but ye have received the Spirit of adoption, whereby we cry Abba Father.* Paul is explaining led by the Spirit, which is the Holy Spirit, God's Chosen, in other words, those who belong to God are Adopted into His Family, the Family of the Church, Royal Priesthood, Peculiar People, God's People, The Sheep, the Children of the Promise, The Saints, The Elect, Believers, Bond Servants, and The Chosen which all mean God's Children. He is now our Father God, and we address Him as such. **The internal or "Effectual Call" is heard and obeyed only by God's Elect. The rest of mankind hear only the "External Call" and go their way, making excuses, even denying God's Sovereignty, and justifying their lifestyles because they love the world and their sin more than God. Unless God opens the eyes, ears, and hearts of the blind, they see only their own selfish desires.** A.W. Pink, an English Bible teacher, once said, *"Multitudes desire to be saved from Hell (The natural instinct of self-preservation) who are quite <u>unwilling</u> to be saved from sin."* This quote sums up and defines the unconverted heart, the condition we all were in before God saved us.

The "U" in T.U.L.I.P. means Unconditional Election. Let's touch on Romans 9:15-16 NLT *For God said to Moses, "I will show mercy to anyone I choose, and I will show compassion to anyone I choose. "So it is God who decides to show mercy.* ***We can neither choose it nor work for it.*** *"* What Paul is saying here is that <u>Salvation is **ALL** of God and His Will alone</u>, not any person's will or person's doings, desires, or their good deeds. It's entirely due to God's Will, which was determined before He created the World; **God is Sovereign, and we are not God**. Salvation is zero percent man and one hundred percent God! <u>Again, 0% man and 100% God, this is extremely, extremely important that you comprehend this; towards your capacity to understand anything in the Bible, particularly if you profess being a Child of God.</u>

John 17:9 NKJV *"I pray for them. I do not pray for the world but for those whom You have given Me, for they are Yours."* Here, Jesus declares yet another of the many Election verses, stating who He is and who He prays for. Jesus does not say He is praying for the world or the lost, but for **His Children; those whom the Father gave to Him,** which was before the foundation of the world. It cannot be clearer than this. R.C. Sproul, theologian, teacher, and Pastor, explains Election in a way many will grasp. *"God just doesn't throw a life preserver to a drowning person. He goes to the bottom of the sea, and pulls a corpse from the bottom of the sea, takes him up on the bank, breathes into him the breath of life, and makes him alive."* As you realize in this quote, dead men don't decide or choose, or accept, (they can't go after any life preserver) or anything, **they're DEAD!** Such is the actual spiritual condition of all people until God opens the Eyes of some, His Elect.

25

The "L" is for Limited Atonement. Let's go to John 10:11,15 KJV *I am the good shepherd: the good shepherd giveth his life for the sheep...As the Father knoweth me even so I the Father and I lay down my life for the sheep.* Notice in these two verses that Jesus is affirming He lays down His Life **only for the Sheep, not for everyone.** Throughout the Bible, the Sheep symbolize God's People, His Elect. Let's look at and dig into John 6:44 NKJV *No one can come to Me unless the Father who sent Me <u>draws</u> him; and I will raise him up at the last day.* Jesus, while preaching, overhears many murmuring at Him, doubting what He is saying, doubting His Deity, His Divinity. So, He speaks clearly to them, explaining why they cannot believe or understand Him: they are **doubting Him because they were not His Children;** The Father did not choose them for the Son. The Greek word <u>drawn here is "Helko," which means to drag; again, as we read previously in Romans 3:11, NO ONE WILL SEEK GOD. He has to drag His Children.</u> **Thank God for such a Loving Father!**

Let's move a little forward, still in John 6:64-65 NLT, *but some of you do not believe me." (For Jesus knew from the beginning which ones didn't believe, and he knew who would betray him.) Then he said, "That is why I said that people can't come to me unless the Father gives them to me."* Here, Jesus is being rejected by many so-called "followers", so **He teaches the hard truths few want to hear.** He tells them that He knows who does not believe Him (those are the lost), who will not be saved later; He is saying what is true. He also knew who would betray Him, and that did not change later either; they were not His. He continues to communicate with the crowds, stating that unless His Father Chose Them (before the foundation of the world), people will not come to Him or follow Him without ceasing, no matter what happens to them. **Genuine Believers recognize we are in God's Hands; He is sovereign, we are not.**

In Matthew 26:28 KJV, Jesus says, *for this is my blood of the New Testament which is shed for* **many** *for the forgiveness of sins.* Jesus makes it clear; He died to save many, <u>not all</u>. Again, each time you read in the Bible, God's Chosen, or The Elect, The Sheep, or His Elect, Holy People, His Treasured People, His Faithful, or a Remnant; these are also terms used in God's Word which identify His Children; those that will spend Eternity with Him.

Jump to John 20:28 KJV *Even as the Son of man came not to be ministered unto, but to minister, and to give his life a ransom for many.* Jesus, while instructing His followers, stated that even He, **God in the flesh**, came to serve others and not to be served, yet He says He gives His Life up for many, <u>not all.</u>

The "I" stands for Irresistible Grace; those whom God has predetermined (Predestined) Will Be Saved. They will not refuse or reject His Salvation or Grace. **Jesus's death on the cross Will Save Everyone It Was Meant to Save, no one else.** Let's unpack Romans 8:30 KJV *...whom he did predestinate, them he also called, and whom he called, them he also justified, and whom he justified, them he also glorified.* Paul is explaining what God has done in a way that we can all understand. God Predestined Us (to mark out, to pick). He Called Us (Chose), then He justified us (removed our sin, past, present, and future, along with its Guilt and penalty) and Proclaimed Us Righteous. He also Glorified Us. Paul uses the past tense as if it happened already, confirming it's inevitable; it's our New Body's Likeness to Christ, which will occur during the Rapture, a Glorified Body for Eternity.

Let's unpack Psalms 115:3 KJV *But our God is in the heavens: he hath done whatsoever he hath pleased.* Here we see what we already know. God can do what He pleases, when He pleases. And therefore, **cannot be resisted in any way, His Will Shall Be Done.** Do you remember Jonah wanting to do as He wished? How did that turn out? More about Jonah in chapter 9.

Go to Job 42:2 NKJV *"I know that You can do everything, And that no purpose of Yours can be withheld from You.* Job surely recognized God's power firsthand. We can apply this understanding to every one of the Elect, **we all will confess, we had nothing to do with our own Salvation,** nor could we resist His love. Let's keep digging...

Look now at 1 John 4:19 KJV: *We love him, because he first loved us.* Here we see the real reason anyone would give up their life for Jesus, because He First Loved Us; it was not the other way around.

Look at Romans 9:16 KJV *So then it is not of him that willeth, nor of him that runneth, but of God that sheweth mercy.* Here, as we unpack this verse, we see Salvation is all God's Will, not ours. If left to my will, I would have never wanted to get to know Him more each day, study His Word each day, pray many, many times each day, tell others of His Grace...write this book. Have you ever noticed that even the Apostles ran when Jesus was arrested and crucified? But **after they received the Holy Ghost in The Upper Room, they all were willing to die professing The Truth**? More on this later, let's keep digging...

Let's head again to Ephesians 2:8-9 KJV. We are looking at this verse again, this time to examine it more deeply. *For by grace are ye saved through faith; and that not of yourselves: it is the gift of God: Not of works, lest any man should boast.* Here we read that we are saved through Faith (which is from God). We, in our own power, cannot muster enough Faith to believe. It again is NOT of Ourselves, and it's a Gift of and from God; remember the definition of "Gift": no one demands a gift, or even asks for one, but one can always beg for Mercy. This way, no one can ever boast or brag that they earned salvation, or that they deserve salvation, or that they were smart or religious enough. Concerning Salvation, there are no good works involved, no amount of Bible studies, no "church" attendance, no walking down "church" aisles, no uttering prayers, no good deeds of any kind, no money given to the poor, no money given to some "church", no being "good" in any "religious" way. Salvation is Only God's Doing and Not Ours, His Choice and its **never based on you or anything you did or will do**. One last verse for this one, go to Ephesians 2:5 NKJV *even when we were dead in trespasses, made us alive together with Christ (by grace you have been saved)* we see here that we are all dead to God, all of us, we cannot rise from the dead, we cannot save ourselves, we must exclusively, entirely rely on God's Mercy.

The "P" represents the Perseverance of the Saints. First, go to Philippians 1:1 KJV *Paul and Timothy, bond servants of Christ Jesus, To all the Saints in Christ Jesus...* Here, Paul is referring to himself and all Believers as Slaves (bond servants), which we are joyfully, and this refers to all Believers as Saints. Saints live forever in the presence of our Lord. Let's unpack **1 John 2:19 KJV** *They went out from us, but they were not of us; for if they had been of us, they would in no doubt have continued with us: but they went out, that they might be made manifest that they were not all of us.* Here, John reveals the spirit of the false convert (those NOT born again by God). The signs of the lost are leaving the faith, denying Christ, **or losing their passion for Jesus.** This reveals the obvious that they were not saved, not genuine followers of Jesus. **Let me ask you, if YOU were following God, and you knew it was God, would you turn and walk**

away? Of course not, only unbelievers would even consider that. Knowing that Jesus is the Holy One, who created the world, created YOU; would you turn and walk away? Think about it...John states that those traveling with them who professed Christ as Lord left them and changed their minds about following them and following Christ; they were the "make-believers." <u>True Believers never leave the Faith and come back to it.</u> If a person is truly Born Again, they want to know God, Jesus, and the Holy Spirit more and more each day through His Word. If you think you came back to Him because you thought you were once saved, you weren't saved before at all; you were like I once was... fooling yourself and others, being a "make-believer."

If you knew you were doing the bidding of God, would you choose not to? Could you give up knowing who your Father was once your eyes were open to Him and His Truths? Of course not, nor would you want to. Let's look at Jeremiah 32:38-40 KJV *And they shall be my people, and I will be their God. I will give them one heart and one way, that they may **fear** me forever, for their own good and the good of their children after them. I will make with them an everlasting covenant that I will not turn away from doing good to them. And I will put the <u>fear of me</u> in their hearts that they may not turn from me.* Here, God speaks through the Prophet Jeremiah, stating that the True Chosen People, Chosen by God Himself, Will Never Leave the Faith that God supplies. God doesn't say in the above verse that He hopes so, or that He can find the right preacher to convince them, or that they might be His People. He Said They Will be His People, Period. He says He Will Give Them One Heart, One Way, Jesus; God places a Fear for Him in Each One, a Fear of Himself. Do you have that? He is a Holy God; we are sinful creatures from the dirt. God adds, "He will make with them an Everlasting

Covenant." He says, "His People Will Never Leave Him or turn from Him, period." If one does, their faith was just a work of the flesh. **Reminding Reader to Refer to Point #1**

Let's unpack a little deeper, go to John 10:26-30 KJV *...but you do not believe because you are not my sheep. My sheep listen to my voice; I know them, and they follow me. I give them eternal life, and they shall never perish; no one will snatch them out of my hand. My Father, who has given them to me, is greater than all; no one can snatch them out of my Father's hand. I and the Father are one."* Here, Jesus is speaking from the Temple in Solomon's porch. He is explaining why many don't understand or believe Him; it's because Jesus came to Save Only His sheep, not the whole world, and not the goats (goats symbolize unrepentant sinners, the lost, the wicked, the natural man). His Chosen Will ALL be Saved, no one can change the Hearts or Minds of the Elect, they will NOT deny Jesus. True Salvation is everlasting, which cannot be thwarted. Some of you may be thinking, but Peter denied Jesus three times. Yes, that was before Peter was given the Holy Spirit in the Upper Room, which was before Christ was raised from the dead. The Holy Spirit is now given to ALL Believers the instant one is Born Again or Saved, (once God reveals His Truths, Himself, and His Mercy, Grace, and Love to you, He gives you His Faith, His Spirit, and you Believe and Repent). The Holy Spirit is the third Person in the Trinity. **God The Father Elects and Preserves Us; God the Son Intercedes for Us; God the Spirit Indwells and Assists Us.**

As for Faith, look at Romans 12:3 NJKV *For I say, through the grace given to me, to everyone who is among you, not to think of himself more highly than he ought to think, but to think soberly, as God has dealt to each one a measure of faith.* Here, Paul explains that **Faith is given by God,** not created in the hearts of men (not through positive thinking), but is dispersed and created by God, given by measure to those who are God's Chosen. Let's look at Romans 10:17 NIV *consequently, faith comes from hearing the message, and the message is heard through the word about Christ.* The Message is The Gospel. Once God opens a believer's heart, ears, and eyes to Him, the Whole Bible Lights Up, and you can't wait to dig in! Keep reading the Word, to yourself or out loud, in "church" or in your home, your Faith will increase whenever you are tested. Continue to believe what God's Word says, and your Faith will continue to grow. **Christ is the Author and Finisher of your Faith. Amen!**

Go over to 1 Peter 2:9 KJV: *But you are a chosen generation, a royal priesthood, an holy nation, a peculiar people; that ye should show forth the praises of him who hath called you out of the darkness into his marvelous light.* Here, Peter is writing to Believers, stating they are God's Own Special People, a **Peculiar People**, and therefore should Praise God! GOD Called Us from our evil thinking, wrong doings, and our lost condition, into His Mercy, His Grace, and His Truth of Light. **This should bring each Believer to his knees**, just realizing how much God has done for each of His Children. Please take a minute to think about this verse. Are YOU praising God through Jesus often?

C.S. Spurgeon once said, *"If someone should ask me what I mean by a **Calvinist**, I should reply, He is one who says, Salvation is of the Lord. I cannot find in Scripture any other doctrine than this. It is the essence of the Bible."* I fully agree with you, my Brother! Let's park here for a minute to dig deeper into **Calvinism**, and we find that John Calvin used the Scriptures rightly and had the correct understanding of Biblical Truths. It is reading The Bible and using Biblical Exegesis to interpret God's Holy Word rightly;

of course, as we explore the Bible, **we see Calvin was correct in his exposition.** The false teachers are the only ones who want to discredit God's Word, as to debunk what God's intentions were and still are, because of personal **pride**, or "church" size, they will always disagree with God's Election. They want to take some credit, some responsibility for their own salvation; those who think that way have a false salvation that is self-induced, that was once me...BUT GOD.

I am not reformed in my Theology because I read John Calvin, C.S. Spurgeon, Martin Luther, R.C. Sproul, or John MacArthur.... I am Reformed in my Theology because I have read THE BIBLE. Spurgeon once said, *"Reformed Theology is nothing more than Biblical Christianity."* And I agree; those who reject such teaching from God's Word reject God's Word, period. Those who would twist Scripture are the ones you want to correct or avoid.

Let's take a look at the "Five Solas," which summarize the Protestant Faith. Protestant (means those who <u>protested</u> against the false teachings of the Catholic church). **All Christians are therefore Protestant.** The "Catholic faith" is nothing more than a well-disguised cult. <u>The Reformer's fundamental belief is that Salvation is by Faith in Christ alone.</u>

The "Five Solas" are five Latin phrases used as a set of principles that emerged from the Protestant Reformation. They summarize the Reformers' basic Theological principles, which contrast with the teachings of the Roman Catholic "Church". "Sola" means "alone" or "only," and these phrases exclude all works or good deeds of man. **Sola fide (by Faith alone), we are saved through Faith alone in Jesus Christ,** which is a Gift from God alone. **Sola Scriptura (by Scripture alone),** The Bible alone is our Highest Authority. Meaning the Bible gives us everything we need for our Theology, God's

Holy Spirit inspires all 66 Books. The Holy Spirit also helps us to understand and obey Scripture. **Solus Christus (through Christ alone)** Jesus Christ alone is our Lord, Savior, and King! We are Only Saved because of what Christ has done; we add nothing to that—**Sola Gratia (Grace alone). The grace of God alone saves us**, and such Grace is God's Gift to His Children. **Soli Deo Gloria (Glory to God alone).** We live for The Glory of God alone. That is the core reason we exist: to give Glory to God alone. These Biblical Truths function as Theological Supports in and of **Our Christian Faith, which is unyielding to any false Doctrine and false teaching.**

Chapter 2: If I am a Good Person, I am Going to Heaven, Right?

I am a good person! This is the number one response when asked, *"Are you going to Heaven when you die, and why?"* Let us address this serious question by starting in Exodus and the 10 Commandments. Which were written with the finger of God on two stone tablets and given to Moses on Mount Sinai; let us see if we can get through them without breaking one. Let's dig in...Exodus 20:3 KJV **(The 1st Commandment)** *Thou shalt have no other gods before me.* This verse eliminates most of the world already. God is saying No other gods before Him. Yet, if we study other religions, they follow a god of their own making, or no god at all, or multiple false gods, not the God of the Holy Bible. The world says we must respect all religions; The Bible says, *"Thou shalt have no other gods before me."* I will go with what God's Word says. We should have NO respect for any other religions; they are all from Satan! Let me ask you a question or two: *"What is your passion?"* or *"What do you think about the most during each day?"* When you give me your answer, will you be honest?

Many have passions for sports, money, careers, houses, buildings, cars, power, comforts, fame, friends, stuff, and more stuff, or even themselves, while to all that I say, "Those are your gods." Whatever you spend the most time thinking about or doing, praising or wanting, that is your god. Do you have any celebrities you want to meet? Do you have any sportspeople you want to meet? Do you look up to them, have their picture on your walls, want their autograph, or know their batting average or points scored? Do you have a team jersey with a player's number? **Those people are your gods... note the small "g".** Have you ever placed anything or a "god" before The God of the Bible? If so, by definition, you are **guilty of idolatry.** Some people today say they can't live without their cell phones; let us continue.

Exodus 20:4-5 KJV **(The 2nd Commandment)** *Thou shalt **not make unto thee any graven image**, or any likeness of anything that is in heaven above, or that is in the earth beneath, or that is in the water under the earth. Thou shalt not bow down thyself to them nor serve them, for I the Lord thy God am a jealous God...* This verse eliminates Catholics, Buddhists, Hindus, false converts, and over 4200 different religions, which are all false. Just having a cross with "Jesus" on it is blasphemy. The statues of Mary are all **blasphemy.** Any statue of anyone someone worships or looks up to in any way is against God and is, of course, blasphemy. **Pictures or any likeness of someone's portrayal of what Jesus looked like is all blasphemy!** This nonsense is only practiced by baby Christians, make-believers, or those who are lost. Let me add, 1 Corinthians 11:14 NIV *Does not the very nature of things teach you that if a man has long hair, it is a disgrace to him,* I am so sick and tired of seeing so-called "Jesus" pictures on social media; I tell those who post such garbage to read The 2nd Commandment. **Jesus did NOT have long hair!** Movies, books, and pictures everywhere show some gay looking hippie freak with long hair and blue eyes. The Truth about Jesus was that He blended in with all the other Jewish men of Isreal that time, in every way, physically. No images means no images, yet I see so many so-called "believers" disgracing and shaming God in this way each day. Enough said. Have you ever looked at a picture or sculpture and prayed to it? If you even have any pictures of "God", "Jesus", or "Satan", or celebrated "Halloween" in any way, then by God's definition, you are **guilty of idolatry.**

Exodus 20:7 KJV **(The 3rd Commandment)** *Thou shalt not take the name of the Lord thy God in vain: for the*

Lord will not hold him guiltless that taketh his name in vain. This verse says we should not take God's name in vain, meaning it's blasphemy to do so. What is taking His Name in vain, you are asking? Have you ever said "G-d-dam" Or "Jesus!" or "Jesus Christ!" when you got mad or stubbed your toe, or to emphasize a statement? **How about movies where they blaspheme God's name countless times each day?** Have you ever said "Oh My God" or texted OMG? These things are not acceptable to God; things unacceptable to God are called sins. One sin omits anyone from Heaven. Are you beginning to see that no one is "good enough" yet? God is Holy, and we need to show deep reverence, deep, deep appreciation and respect, even Fear of Him. Let's go to Matthew 10:28 KJV. Jesus is speaking *Do not be afraid of those who kill the body but cannot kill the soul. Rather, be afraid of the One who can destroy both soul and body in Hell.* Here, Jesus makes it clear that we should fear God; fear is the beginning of knowledge. Proverbs 1:7 KJV *The fear of the Lord is the beginning of knowledge: but fools despise wisdom and instruction.* We need to take God and sin very, very seriously. God took it so seriously that He sent Jesus to die for it, to save some! Have you ever taken the name of the Lord in vain? Then by definition, you are **guilty of blasphemy.**

Exodus 20:8 KJV **(The 4th Commandment)** *Remember the Sabbath day, to keep it holy.* God is saying you should labor six days but rest on the seventh, make it Holy (set apart for God's use). This does not apply to the New Testament Believer, yet the other nine commandments still do. It's Colossians 2:16 KJV, Paul is teaching here. *Let no man therefore judge you in meat, or in drink, or in respect of an holyday, or of the new moon, or of the Sabbath days:* Yet we should chose a day each week to rest and attend a

Reformed Church, one (believing the whole Bible, which denies the Catholic theology and the "Arminian theology" more on this later). Find a Bible-believing church so that you may grow in your understanding and Faith through the study of God's Word. The 1800's English Evangelical Anglican Bishop J.C. Ryle said, *"Never forget that Truth is more important to a Church than Peace" (More on all this distinction later).* Let's take a quick look at 2 Timothy 2:15 KJV: *Study to show thyself approved unto God, a workman that needeth not to be ashamed, rightly dividing the word of truth.* Here, we see Paul in his 2nd letter to Timothy explaining **the need to study God's Word, not merely read it.** I always make the comparison to Algebra; we don't read Algebra, we study it. Let's bounce over to Psalms 1:1-2, ESV, written by King David. *Blessed is the man who walks not in the counsel of the wicked, nor stands in the way of sinners, nor sits in the seat of scoffers; but his delight is in the law of the Lord, and on his law he meditates day and night.* Such a person agrees with what God calls sin and will not compromise God's Truths to blend in or be accepted by the wicked (unsaved, those who are of this world), but finds joy in God's laws and meditates on them day and night. What is it that occupies your mind most of the day? What or who do you meditate on? **The Lord is on a Christian's Mind throughout the day, every day.**

Let's continue to Exodus 20:12 KJV **(The 5ᵗʰ Commandment)** *Honor thy father and thy mother: that thy days may be long upon the land which the Lord thy God giveth thee.* Here God is saying, "Honor your mother and father, and you shall live long (grow old)". The good thing about the Ten Commandments is that they are very clear to all, and there is no confusion with God. Today's child seems to run their parents' household, with their whining, complaining, and demanding rights that don't exist. They constantly yell and talk back to their parents, as if they were in charge. There is little to no respect for children in most American households today. Even in Christian families, some grow up and go off to college, and if their faith is weak or fake, that will be fully exposed when they get back home. If they blended in at college rather than stood out for Christ's sake, you will see the fruit, or lack of it. If they no longer follow the Teachings of God's Word, it's because they were away from those who were teaching them morals and scripture; therefore, once removed from such guidance, the true self is exposed. They were not born again, yet seemed to be before college days. **The secular colleges of today will destroy a mind rather than build one, concerning morals and God's Truths.** There's a liberal mindset, taught in schools today and by the media, and **one can never become a liberal by reading and studying the Bible**. This is a cause-and-effect situation. Parents today are frightened to discipline their own kids; let's face it, most parents watch fake news, and their minds are not on God.

Let's go to Proverbs 13:24 ESV: *Whoever spares the rod hates his son, but he who loves him is diligent to discipline him.* In most households today, parents are afraid that their child would call the police and have them arrested if they try to discipline their own children. If I tried that, my mother would have broken my fingers, and rightly so. My Dad only hit me once; I understood respect for them at a young age, although my mom threw an accurately aimed slipper often! Let's jump over to Proverbs 22:6 KJV *Train up a child in the way he should go: and when he is old, he will not depart from it.* This is not always available in every home, yet it should be. When schools in America removed Prayer and the reading of the Bible, there was a destructively negative effect on all households in America. Yet the home is where we must teach our children Godly values and train them for life by studying the Bible, even a few verses each day to start. Have you ever dishonored one of your parents? By definition, you are **guilty of breaking God's law.**

Moving forward to Exodus 20:13 ESV **(The 6ᵗʰ Commandment)** *"You shall not murder."* I used the English Standard Version here because it more closely describes this Commandment, and throughout this book, I have used several different versions of the Bible to enhance clarity. The Hebrew word "murder" also covers human death through carelessness or negligence. Murder is the unlawful killing of another, the intentional, premeditated killing with malice. Here God is saying murder is not okay, yet in self-defense, or in preventing a person from murdering another seemingly innocent person, or in the case of someone breaking into your home, these are exceptions. Let's hop over to Exodus 22:2 NIV: *If a thief is caught breaking in at night and is struck a fatal blow, the defender is not guilty of bloodshed.* As we see here in Exodus, and there are other verses also that support self-defense, **if a killing occurs in an attempt to save the life of an innocent person, that is not murder.** The difference between the illegal and legal use of deadly force, whether with a weapon or by hand, turns on intent, justification, and motive, and these distinctions are explained throughout the scriptures. And concerning war, let's start in Ecclesiastes 3:3,8 KJV: *A time to kill, and a time to heal; a time to break down, and a time to build up... A time to love, and a time to hate; a time of war, and a time of peace.* Here we read that there is a time for all things, even war. There are many battles in the Bible, some of which God commands; killing armed combatants who are out to kill you, in itself, is not sinful. Wars are inevitable and Biblical. Let's take a jog over to 1 John 3:15 KJV *Whosoever hateth his brother is a murderer: and ye know that no murderer hath eternal life abiding in him.* Here, John is stating that even hating someone in your heart by God's standards is considered murder. Have you ever hated someone in your heart? Here you see that no one who has **any hate** in their heart could inherit eternal life; if you have, you are, **by God's definition, a murderer.**

Let's move to Exodus 20:14 KJV **(The 7ᵗʰ Commandment)** *Thou shall not commit adultery.* This seems plain and easy to understand, but let's see what Jesus says in Matthew 5:27-28 KJV. Ye *have heard that it was said by them of old time, Thou shalt not commit adultery: But I say unto you, That whosoever **looketh on a woman to lust after** her, hath committed adultery with her already in his heart.* Seems the bar is raised a lot here; this applies to both men and women. This means that a woman lusting after any man other than her husband or any man at any time is also a sin. Let's take a moment here to clarify marriage. Go to Genesis 2:24 KJV, *therefore shall a man leave his father and his mother, and shall cleave unto his wife: and they shall be one flesh.* Notice that God says man should have one wife, not multiple wives (as some cultures condone), and that **the two become one.** This is where our math doesn't work, but God's math does. Skip over to 1 Corinthians 7:2 KJV *Nevertheless, to avoid fornication, let every man have his own wife, and let every woman have her own husband.* This is clear again: it's a man and a woman, never a man with a man or a woman with a woman. This is not a joke...back to the 7th Commandment, if you are a man, have you ever looked at a woman with lust? And if you're a woman, have you ever looked at a man and lusted after him? Then you are, by God's definition and God's standards, **an adulterer.** Give the book **"The Guide to Christian Dating, Marriage, and Sex"** a read.

Let's go to Exodus 20:15 KJV **(The 8th Commandment)** *Thou shalt not steal.* This one seems easy and clear, you might say. Let me ask you, have you ever taken anything that was not yours, possibly a pen from work, something from your job that wouldn't be missed? Maybe you took candy as a kid, or food that wasn't yours because you were hungry? Any dishonest act that gets you something that you shouldn't receive is stealing. Let's visit 2 Thessalonians 3:10 NKJV *For even when we were with you, we commanded you this: If anyone will not work, neither shall he eat.* Here, we find Paul instructing the Thessalonians to withdraw from the disorderly and the lazy among them. Have you ever stolen anything? If so, then **you are a thief** by definition.

Let's move to Exodus 20:16 KJV **(The 9th Commandment)** *Thou shalt not bear false witness against thy neighbor.* This mainly means telling the truth. Do you always tell the truth? Have you always told the truth and nothing but the truth? Let's look at Acts 5:1-11 NLT: *but there was a certain man named Ananias who, with his wife, Sapphira, sold some property. He brought part of the money to the apostles, <u>claiming it was the full amount. With his wife's consent</u>, he kept the rest. Then Peter said, "Ananias, why have you let Satan fill your heart? You lied to the Holy Spirit, and you kept some of the money for yourself. The property was yours to sell or not sell, as you wished. And after selling it, the money was also yours to give away. How could you do a thing like this? You weren't lying to us but to God!" As soon as Ananias heard these words, he fell to the floor and died. Everyone who heard about it was terrified. Then some young men got up, wrapped him in a sheet, and took him out and buried him. About three hours later his wife came in, not knowing what had happened. Peter asked her, "Was this the price you and your husband received for your land?" "Yes," she replied, "that was the price." And Peter said, "How could the two of you even think of conspiring to test the Spirit of the Lord like this? The young men who buried your husband are just outside the door, and they will carry you out, too." Instantly, she fell to the floor and died. When the young men came in and saw that she was dead, they carried her out and buried her beside her husband. Great fear gripped the entire church and everyone else who heard what had happened.* This is how God handled a husband and wife, who <u>lied</u> (about the amount of money they sold their property for). God struck them both dead. Imagine if He did that today, would you be left standing? **Sin wouldn't be so attractive if the wages were paid immediately**. Do you see that no one can be perfect but Jesus? We are all sinners in need of a Savior. <u>Have you ever lied to anyone? Then by definition, **you are a liar.**</u>

Let's move to Gods **(10th Commandment),** Exodus 20:17 NIV: *You shall not covet your neighbor's house. You shall not covet your neighbor's wife, or his male or female servant, his ox or donkey, or anything that belongs to your neighbor.* Let's unpack this last Commandment. God is saying, don't desire, covet, or long for another person's stuff, or house, or his wife, or his servants if he or she has any. In other words, don't be envious, don't crave or desire another's goods or their stature, their looks, or their money, be happy for those that have, and pray or give help to others in need, if you are able. **Just wanting something that is not yours is a sin as well.** Are you now convinced that neither you nor I can be without sin? Now you see, on our own merits, we are not good enough for God. God demands only sinless perfection. Only His Son, Jesus the Christ, could and has already passed this test. **Never compare yourself to others who call themselves "Christians," compare yourself to Scripture. Compare yourself to Jesus.**

Chapter 3: Does God Love and Hate People?

This is an interesting question that, at first glance, most would say: God loves everyone. Then why is there a Hell that God sends most to? Let's check out Matthew 5:44-46 NKJV *But I say to you, love your enemies, bless those who curse you, do good to those who hate you, and pray for those who spitefully use you and persecute you, that you may be sons of your Father in heaven; for He makes His sun rise on the evil and on the good, and sends rain on the just and on the unjust. For if you love those who love you, what reward have you? Do not even the tax collectors do the same?* Here, Jesus explains that a Believer's love should be like God's. Jesus acknowledges that many will curse you and persecute you, love them anyway. This love is not about hanging out with people who hate or despise us, but about remembering that we may once have been a hater, before God opened our eyes to know His Son. You see, God brings up the sun each day; it's beautiful, it's majestic, and the moonlight, wow, what a joy to see! This is for all people, so in this way God loves everyone (common grace). He supplies air to breathe, He gives life and created this world, in that way, yes God loves, for He is good all the time. Let's continue to dig...

Let me tell you about an incident I had years ago while working on the 2nd Poetry book, **"God's Clarity through Poetry 2."** Get a copy! I was at a gym in Central Florida. There was a hairstylist named Ron who had his shop at that gym. I went in, sat down, and got a haircut. I talked about the Gospel, and he seemed to be a believer as far as I could tell, in such a short time. But he cut my hair much too short, and in my mind, I vowed never to let him cut my hair ever again. Months went by; again, I was at that gym. I was there about 5 days a week. One day, I had the desire to go back and sit in Ron's chair for another haircut. I dismissed the thought, saying to myself, "No way," but as I walked out the gym door that day, something made me turn around. So, I went in, hoping Ron was not there, but he was. So, I sat down reluctantly, and immediately I knew why I was prompted to sit back in Ron's chair. Ron told me he was getting a divorce. He went on to say how he and his wife are ready to just do it. I listened to him and then replied, "God never advocated divorce; God hates divorce." He was and is against it, but because of the people's hard-heartedness, Moses allowed it. And I continued on for about ten minutes. He was not moved; his mind was still set on a divorce. I said to him, "Ron, can you give me your e-mail address? I have a Poem you and your wife need to read together entitled, "**Love Even Though.**" I said to him, "The poem I will e-mail you will be in my next Poetry book." I said that because he had my first book and said he loved it! He said, "Of course". And he gave me his e-mail address, and that day when I got home, I e-mailed a copy of that poem to him immediately.

I thought nothing of it; time went by. I just kept going to the gym as usual. About 3 weeks later, while I was parking my car to go to the gym, I was rather far away; it was a busy parking lot. As I got out of my car, I saw Ron on his cell phone by the gym's front door. Once he saw me, he immediately put away his cell phone and ran towards me. I was baffled as to why; let me give you some of my background. I studied five styles of Martial Arts over a 20-year span; I boxed as an amateur and was undefeated, then trained for 3 years to turn pro. I even wrote a book back in 1995 titled **"The Bible on How to Box,"** which covered street self-defense, and I taught private lessons back then to make ends meet. Let me stop here. So, I was thinking: while Ron was running towards me, would I have to block or duck his punch or kick? I was confused about why he would be mad at me. If he had something to say, why couldn't he wait until I got to the door, since I was on my way into the gym anyway? All these thoughts were on my mind at the same time. But Ron obviously could not wait that day; he ran fast right up to me... and hugged me! Yes, hugged me! He said, *"Wow, man, you saved my marriage!"* He excitedly continued, *"Both of us read that poem you sent, it had my wife and me crying for hours, bro! You saved our marriage."* I said, *"Wow, and thank you, but God saved your marriage!"* Sometimes just a poem

45

with Biblical connotations or **God's Truths can turn a heart or two back toward God and His Mercy, His Grace**, His overwhelming Love to make and keep two, one! Two who could go back to the day they were married and rekindle their love, with the help of Jesus. **Yes, God used a mere poem to help keep them together, but it was all Him.** I brought up this story in this book to show you, the reader, just how simple it is for things done on behalf of God to work toward His Kingdom agenda. We all have a part to play while we are here for a little while. You can give out bible tracks, Gospels of John, talk to many, write a book, or even a poem or two, and God may use it. **What are you doing currently to further God's kingdom agenda?**

The most popular verse in the Bible and the next two verses that follow, John 3:16-18 KJV *For God so loved the world, that he gave his only begotten Son, that whosoever believeth in him should not perish, but have everlasting life. For God sent not his Son into the world to condemn the world; but that the world through him might be saved. He that believeth on him is not condemned: but he that believeth not is condemned already, because he hath not believed in the name of the only begotten Son of God.* God loves so much that He gave His Own Son up to be scourged, beaten, tortured, and then crucified; so, to say God does not love is a complete lie. He Loves with a Love that is Pure Charity, Pure Grace and Pure Mercy. There is No Comparison to God's Love; it is Everlasting and Forever Forgiving. This also says in verses 17-18 that He condemns (throws into Hell) all those who don't believe. Therefore, whenever someone brings up the verse John 3:16, I remind them that no one should ever take any verse out of context and manipulate and or abuse it. The Bible was written without any verses; they were all added in the 16th century to help us navigate The Word of God. I am hoping that fact will bring new understanding to some. I always ask those who use this verse (John 3:16), *"Did you read the next two verses?"* Then I say to them, *"Okay, let's look now at Revelations 3:16 KJV."* So then, because thou art *lukewarm, and neither cold nor hot, I will spue thee out of my mouth.*

Here, Jesus states what the true state is of most so-called "believers" who are simply, in reality, make-believers. Being cold spiritually is to be useless for God, which means not on fire for God and His Truths, only lukewarm, not really walking with Him, not truly obeying His Commandments daily; being cavalier with "your salvation," you are a "lukewarm Christian." **"Lukewarm Christians" are not Christians, but think they are.** If you belittle God's Priceless Mercy and His Incomparable Grace, seeming nonchalant in your life, your attitude regarding God as not being first in your life, which is noticeable by you being disobedient to His Word, then you are not Born Again, period. Jesus says, He will reject you with disgust; He will spit you "vomit" you out of His Mouth, which means He will send you into everlasting torment in Hell. You don't want to be a "lukewarm Christian." To Love Jesus is to Fear and Obey Him; and be Hot for Him and be a Disciple that can't wait to Serve Jesus each day, here and in Heaven! God is a Loving Father.

But let's look at the side of Him that is also a Righteous Judge, being a Righteous Judge, He Cannot Lie, He Cannot go against His Own Nature. He is Holy, Honest, and must do the Right Thing by each person who was ever born and those that are yet to be born. You may ask what the right thing is. In front of a Holy and Righteous God, we are all sinners, and no sin is allowed in Heaven; we are conceived in sin. So where does that leave us? Give the Book, **"It's All Subject to God's Word,"** a read

We went through the Ten Commandments and noticed we are all full of sin! The right thing to do is put everyone in Hell to pay for our own sins. That is correct by God and is His penalty for sin. **And we ALL deserve HELL.** If someone killed your friend and you were sure, but the judge let him out of jail, and didn't give him a life sentence or execution for his crime, you would be very upset! Well, we all killed Jesus on that cross, the entire human race; yes, as if we were yelling for His crucifixion, we killed Jesus. <u>Our very sins</u> killed Jesus, yours and mine. God's rage against sin is part of His Glory; if you look at how God allowed Jesus to be nailed to that cross, and **if you don't see God's wrath against sin there, you are not seeing the absolute love of God there either.** He is all Love, All the Time, yet He Will Always Hate Sin, so much He endured, even orchestrated Jesus's death. Jonathan Edwards, a theologian from the 1700's, said, *"Never did God so manifest His hatred of sin as in the death and sufferings of His only begotten Son."*

Let's dig into Romans 5:6-10 NKJV: *for when we were still without strength, in due time Christ died for the ungodly. For scarcely for a righteous man will one die; yet perhaps for a good man someone would even dare to die. But God demonstrates His own love toward us, in that while we were still sinners, Christ died for us. Much more then, having now been justified by His blood, we shall be saved from wrath through Him. For if when we were enemies we were reconciled to God through the death of His Son, much more, having been reconciled, we shall be saved by His life.* Here, Paul is opening the window of God's Love toward His People, when we were totally helpless in our sinful nature, blind and deaf to Him, His Mercy, His Grace, and His Charity at the right time, Jesus died. Paul continues explaining that even if there was such a man who is righteous, one that is worth dying for, which we are not, but Jesus died when we were all His Enemies, reconciling many to Him. This original disconnect with God was severed by Adam in the Garden of Eden. Jesus (the 2nd Adam) by His Death on the cross and His Resurrection from the dead re-established a link, by rejoining and creating a new connection to God, through Jesus the Christ (Jesus the Messiah), and only through Him. This connection then includes The Father and The Holy Ghost, establishing the rebirth of many, thus the expression and the meaning of being Born Again.

Let's look at 1 Peter 3:18 NIV *For Christ also suffered once for sins, the righteous for the unrighteous, to bring you to God. He was put to death in the body but made alive in the*

Spirit. Here, Peter explains that Christ suffered unjustly and died once, making it a final sacrifice for sins. By doing so, He did away with the Old Testament Covenant of repeating blood sacrifices by the Jewish people for their sins, which only covered sins temporarily, but the death of Christ covers all believers' sins permanently for all eternity. Jesus, having no sin nature, was able to take the place of sinners, the Righteous, which refers to Him for the unrighteous, which refers to us. Such a sacrifice made it possible for Believers to also be Made Alive with Him and In Him.

Think back to the 2nd chapter, where we examined the Ten Commandments. Did you pass the test? Are you sin-free and perfect? No, so you must pay God's Penalty for breaking His Laws, His Commandments; the penalty is everlasting torment in Hell. These are His Rules, and He is God; we are only creatures from the dirt, His Creation. We are not gods. Yet we seek justice, **God's justice places us all in Hell, we don't want His Justice, we want His Mercy!**

Proverbs 16:4 KJV *The Lord hath made all things for himself: yea, even the wicked for the day of evil.* Psalms 145:20 KJV *The Lord preserves all who love him, but all the wicked he will destroy.* Let's unpack these two verses; they say what they say and do not say what they do not say. God has created all things for Himself; He will not share His Glory with any man or anything. He created the Saved and created the heathen, and He says **He will keep the Saved for Himself, and they are for His Son Jesus in Heaven, and the wicked He will torture in Hell for eternity.** Who are the wicked, you ask? Psalms 11:5 ESV *The Lord tests the righteous, but his soul hates the wicked and <u>the one who loves violence</u>.* Psalms 5:5 NLT *Therefore, the proud may not stand in your presence, for you hate all who do evil.* Genesis NLT 6:5 *The Lord observed the extent of human wickedness on the earth, and he saw that everything they thought or imagined was consistently and totally evil.* I guess you realize by now, **God loves and God hates**, and He hates those who are evil or do evil, which are all of us, we are the wicked; unless God the <u>Father sees Christ in us</u>. Let's see Proverbs 6:16-19 NIV

There are six things the Lord hates, seven that are detestable to him: proud eyes, a lying tongue, hands that shed innocent blood, a heart that devises wicked schemes, feet that are quick to rush into evil, a false witness who pours out lies and a person who stirs up conflict in the community. Here God is against those who are proud, those who lie, and those who kill the innocent, as in abortion, those who are crooked, cheaters, and those who seek to be delinquents, thugs, gang bangers, hoodlums, lawbreakers, criminals, and those who are trouble makers, those who are without The Living God, Jesus. Are you living in habitual un-repented sin? Turn and repent of your sins, even the sin of unbelief, and cry out continuously to Jesus. **He's the only hope any of us have.**

Earlier, I stated God Hates, unless He sees Christ in us. What did I mean? It's true, let's confirm that you now understand, God Hates and Loves; see Romans 9:11-24 NIV. *Yet, before the twins were born or had done anything good or bad in order that God's purpose in election might stand: not by works but by him who calls she was told, "The older will serve the younger." Just as it is written: "Jacob I loved, but Esau I hated." What then shall we say? Is God unjust? Not at all! For he says to Moses, "I will have mercy on whom I have mercy, and I will have compassion on whom I have compassion." It does not, therefore, depend on human desire or effort, but on God's mercy. For Scripture says to Pharaoh: "I raised you up for this very purpose, that I might display my power in you and that my name might be proclaimed in all the earth." Therefore God has mercy on whom he wants to have mercy, and he hardens whom he wants to harden. One of you will say to me: "Then why does God still blame us? For who is able to resist his will?" But who are you, a human being, to talk back to God? "Shall what is formed say to the one who formed it, 'Why did you make me like this?' "Does not the potter have the right to make out of the same lump of clay some pottery for special purposes and some for common use? What if God, although choosing to show his wrath and make his power known, bore with great patience the objects of his wrath-prepared for destruction? What if he did this to make the riches of his glory known to the objects of his mercy, whom he prepared in advance for glory, even us, whom he also called, not only from the Jews but also from the Gentiles?*

This is the most revealing chapter into God's Mind. Earlier, I said, *"If God sees Christ in Us, what do I mean?"* Let's unpack and dig deep into the above 13 verses. God says here that He chooses His Children Before Their Birth, yes, long before it. Let's jump again over to Ephesians 1:4 NLT *Even before he made the world, God loved us and chose us in Christ to be holy and without fault in his eyes.* This says, God Chose Us, His Elect, in Christ, not in ourselves; to be set apart (Holy) for His Use, and He therefore will see no fault in us. So, in chapter 13, God says, *"It is written, Jacob I loved, but Esau I hated."* He is relating here a prime example of His Sovereign Grace and <u>His Willful Election</u> as it relates to His final judgment. It also communicates His Love and His Certainty for those He Predetermined before He created this universe. But don't miss this; it also places His Divine Love, Mercy, and Grace on full display! Ask yourself, why would He love Jacob? It's not that He saw anything good in him; Jacob was a liar, a trickster, and he deceived his own brother to gain the blessings of his father, Isaac. But **the true reasons behind God's Election are not known by man.**

Paul goes on to explain the true attributes of God by declaring that **God will have Mercy on whom He wants to, and not who wants Him to.** Think about that for a moment. He further explains in terms we can understand that a potter (one who creates objects from clay) can form that clay in any way he wants; shouldn't God be able to create in the same way? Of course, and He does, He goes on to say **God creates**

some people for good and some not for good. God hardens hearts and softens them. **To question God is absurd; no one knows God's Ways or the inner thoughts of God.** It's Isaiah 55:8-9 NIV: *"For my thoughts are not your thoughts, neither are your ways my ways," declares the Lord. "As the heavens are higher than the earth, so are my ways higher than your ways and my thoughts than your thoughts.* What we do know is what He wants us to know; His Holy Word, and we need to rightly divide it, and not misquote Him or misunderstand His Meanings expressed by Him in The Bible. Matthew 4:4 KJV *But he answered and said, It is written, Man shall not live by bread alone, but by every word that proceedeth out of the mouth of God.* Here, Jesus is rebuking Satan after spending 40 days and 40 nights fasting. Jesus was very weak, yet He knew what truly mattered, which was God's Word, nothing else! Jesus was quoting Deuteronomy 8:3 (remember, Jesus wrote the Bible) and also created Satan. He was 100% man and 100% God, "The God Man," more on His Divinity later. **You will experience an intimate relationship between your affection for Christ and your affection for the Scriptures, for they are One of them same.**

Let's keep digging now: it's Hebrews 12:6-8 KJV *For whom the Lord loveth he chasteneth, and scourgeth every son whom he receiveth. If ye endure chastening, God dealeth with you as with sons; for what son is he whom the father chasteneth not? But if ye be without chastisement, whereof all are partakers, then are ye bastards, and not sons.* Here we read that God loves His Children (which are ALL adopted) and when any parent or Father loves his child, he punishes him when he or she is doing wrong, he corrects his child. He doesn't give a "time out" or take away his or her cell phone, although that in itself may be a good start; he makes the

DIGGING DEEPER INTO GOD'S TRUTH DEFINES A "CHRISTIAN"   JOSEPH MALARA

child feel the pain of the wrong. Scourging was a severe beating possibility with a whip; my mom used hangers or slippers.

The writer of Hebrews goes on to say that if a father does not discipline his child, it's because that child is an illegitimate child, one that is not his or even worthy of correction. **If you don't feel God's Reprove, His Rebuke, or His Correction in your life, then how could you possibly know of His Love?** Let's take it a step further: having **someone who cares enough to correct you is having someone who loves you**; someone who cares that you grow in Truth. When a Christian grows in God's Truths, this Christian needs to share ALL he or she has learned with those they love; (this will cause division). **Doctrine divides truth from error.** Knowledge of God's Word is eternal; therefore, His Truths must be given joyfully and generously to all who can hear. **Life is short, eternity is forever, and so which should be of most importance?**

Many ask why bad things happen to good people. Romans 3:12 says **there are no good people.** We should rather ask why anything good happens to evil, wicked, rebellious sinners like us. That's why God sent His Son...keep digging...

Chapter 4: Is Heaven Real and Is the Bible the Word of God?

Let's dig in and explore this widely talked-about subject. Many ask, *"Is Heaven a Real Place, and how do I know? The Bible is God's Word?"* Why would I put these two questions in one Chapter you might ask? What does God's Word say about all this? These two questions are on the minds of all unbelievers and some believers as well. Let's clear up all this confusion. With so many false religions out there and so many false teachers in the Christian faith alone, how then can anyone be certain that the Bible is the Word of God? There are 40 authors of the Bible, dating back to about 1400 BC (before Christ). The Old Testament was written in Hebrew, and the New Testament in Greek; it was completed around 90 AD (after His death). There was a 400-year gap between the last book of the Old Testament, Malachi, and the first book of the New Testament, Matthew. The Bible is one Book made up of 66 books over about 1600 years in 13 different countries and on 3 continents. It never contradicts itself; it is accurate in every way, Historically, Scientifically, Morally, Doctrinally, and in Prophecy. It is the best-selling book each year, and is The Living Word to those Who Believe. Notice 1400 BC (Before Christ) and 90 AD (After Dead) even our time is judged and calculated by Jesus Birth and His Physical Death at Calvary, which would be about 33 AD. Many never seem to comprehend or recognize even this simple factual information. The Bible uses the Bible to prove it's right, let's see how that all works.

Let's go to 2 Timothy 3:16 AMP *All Scripture is God-breathed [given by divine inspiration] and is profitable for instruction, for conviction [of sin], for correction [of error and restoration to obedience], for training in righteousness [learning to live in conformity to God's will, both publicly and privately—behaving honorably with personal integrity and moral courage];* **Here we see that ALL scripture is God Breathed or Inspired by God.** And it is certainly useful to teach, rebuke, and correct everyone in every way, and that is an understatement. So, if God moved and, in essence, inspired the Whole Bible, He Wrote It. And God, Jesus, and the Holy Spirit are all in Agreement, so each takes credit for this Incredible Living Book. So yes, **Jesus, in a way, wrote the Whole Bible.**

Let's jump back to Genesis 1:26 KJV *Then God said, "Let Us make man in Our image, according to Our likeness; let them have dominion over the fish of the sea, over the birds of the air, and over the cattle, over all the earth and over every creeping thing that creeps on the earth."* Do you notice the word "US" then "OUR"? Here God the Father is In Unison with the Son and the Holy Ghost, all Three Agree, as they have throughout Scripture, the three are One, One Godhead, Three Persons, each equal in Their Divinity. Look at 2 Corinthians 13:14 KJV *The grace of the Lord Jesus Christ, and the love of God, and the communion of the Holy Ghost, be with you all. Amen.* Here, Paul points out the Godhead: **All Three, The Son Jesus, The Father God, and The Holy Spirit.** Check out Colossians 2:9 NIV *For in Christ all the fullness of the Deity lives in bodily form.* Here we read Paul explaining that, in Christ, in human form, God is fully represented, and that the Father and the Holy Ghost are fully represented as well.

Let's look at Matthew 28:19 KJV *Go ye therefore, and teach all nations, baptizing them in the name of the Father, and of the Son, and of the Holy Ghost:* Here, Jesus is explaining **The Great Commission** to His Disciples. To teach and Baptize Believers in The Name of the Father, the Son, and the Holy Ghost, three persons, one Godhead. Jump over now to Matthew 3:16-17 KJV *When He had been baptized, Jesus came up immediately from the water; and behold, the heavens were opened to Him, and He saw the Spirit of God descending like a dove and alighting upon Him. And suddenly a voice came from heaven, saying, "This is My beloved Son, in whom I am well pleased."* Here, Jesus is getting baptized by John the Baptist, and All Three Godheads were present at the same time.

Flip over to John 14:5-9 NKJ *Thomas said to Him, "Lord, we do not know where You are going, and how can we know the way?" Jesus said to him, "I am the way, the truth, and the life. No one comes to the Father except through Me. "If you had known Me, you would have known My Father also; and from now on you know Him and have seen Him." Philip said to Him, "Lord, show us the Father, and it is sufficient for us." Jesus said to him, "Have I been with you so long, and yet you have not known Me, Philip? He who has seen Me has seen the Father; so how can you say, 'Show us the Father'?* Here, Jesus clears up any confusion among His Apostles; He explains that He is the Only Way to The Father God and that <u>Jesus is the human form, God Incarnate.</u>

What I'm exposing here is that the Bible makes complete sense and comes together in countless ways. <u>Most scholars agree that there are over 300 prophecies about Jesus in the Old Testament that have already come true.</u> That is another book within itself. Let's continue with Job 26:7 NLT *God stretches the northern sky over empty space and hangs the earth on nothing.* How would Job know that the earth hung in space with nothing holding it? When Job lived, there was no space travel and no such knowledge; it was ALL God working through the Holy Spirit. Now look at Isaiah 40:22 KJV *It is he that sitteth upon the circle of the earth, and the inhabitants thereof are as grasshoppers; that stretcheth out the heavens as a curtain, and spreadeth them out as a tent to dwell in:* How does Isaiah know this you ask, well he doesn't but God does, and His Words came out of Isaiah. A circle here refers to a globe or sphere; **only the Creator would know such.**

Over the past two thousand years since the death of Jesus, countless lives have been changed and totally impacted through the Power of God by those using and obeying His Word, including America, with its countless blessings, which are due in large part, if not entirely, to God and His Mercy, because we were founded on Judeo-Christian values. I think it's best to let you read part of a sermon by C.H. Spurgeon; it hits the ball out of the park! *"A great many learned men are defending the Gospel; no doubt it is a very proper and right thing to do, yet I always notice that, when there are most books of that kind, it is because the Gospel itself is not being preached. Suppose a number of persons were to take it into their heads that they had to defend a Lion, a full-grown king of beasts! There he is in the cage, and here come all the soldiers of the army to fight for him. Well, I should suggest to them, if they would not object, and feel that it was humbling to them, that they should kindly stand back, open the door, and let the Lion out! I believe that would be the best way of defending him, for he would take care of himself, and the best "apology" for the Gospel is to let the Gospel out. Never mind defending Deuteronomy or the whole of the Pentateuch (the first five books of the Bible); preach Jesus Christ and Him crucified. Let the Lion out, and see who will dare to approach him. The Lion of the tribe of Judah will soon drive away all His adversaries."*

There are many books written defending the Bible as God's Divine Word, and rightfully so. I ask you, the one reading this, if you yourself read The Gospel of John and, after clearly reading and studying what you read, you find your eyes closed to what is being said; read it again and again until God opens your eyes and ears to Him. Cry out to Him over and over again; this may be what He is waiting for you or is orchestrating on your behalf. Study The Gospel of John over and over, **let the Lion out!**

Let's talk of Heaven 1 Peter 1:4 KJV *To an inheritance incorruptible, and undefiled, and that fadeth not away, reserved in heaven for you.* Here we find Peter writing to Believers, giving them a glimpse at what's to come. Remember, Peter was there at the Transfiguration, Matthew 17:1-9 NIV: *Now after six days Jesus took Peter, James, and John his brother, led them up on a high mountain by themselves; and He was transfigured before them. His face shone like the sun, and His clothes became as white as the light. And behold, Moses and Elijah appeared to them, talking with Him. Then Peter answered and said to Jesus, "Lord, it is good for us to be here; if You wish, let us make here three tabernacles: one for You, one for Moses, and one for Elijah." While he was still speaking, behold, a bright cloud* *overshadowed them; and suddenly a voice came out of the cloud, saying, **"This is My beloved Son, in whom I am well pleased. Hear Him!"** And when the disciples heard it, they fell on their faces and were greatly afraid. But Jesus came and touched them and said, "Arise, and do not be afraid." When they had lifted up their eyes, they saw no one but Jesus only. Now as they came down from the mountain, Jesus commanded them, saying, "Tell the vision to no one until the Son of Man is risen from the dead."*

Let me start with **WOW** and **WOW**! You should read this a few times. Here we see that **Jesus shared a glimpse of His True Nature,** a look at His Divinity, His Glory, and a look into the future for the three Apostles with Him. Oh, what a sight this must have been, and hearing God the Father from the clouds tell them who Jesus truly was! Such confirmation of Jesus coming from Heaven and a confirmation that the Prophets of the Old Testament, Moses and Elijah, were in their Spiritual Bodies Alive! **This is confirmation and validation within itself of ALL of God's Word, Old and New Testament!**

The Bible is the True and Living Word of God. 1 Corinthians 1:18 NKJV *For the message of the cross is foolishness to those who are perishing, but to us who are being saved it is the power of God.* Here we see that Paul exposes the cold, hard truth. Remember, there are 66 books in the Bible, all historical (all happened) except one, which is yet to come, The Book of Revelation. God's Truths are All Absolute; such is Truth itself. Give the book, **"Examine The End Times,"** a read

Let's look at the American diet, and I use this comparison as an analogy of today's average "Christian" couple; they attend a "church" on Sunday. Then go to a fast-food restaurant after "church." This couple meets and eats at the same fast-food restaurant each day of their workweek. They order their meal, i.e., a double hamburger with ketchup, large fries, and a diet soda, thinking they are doing their bodies well. Why would they think any differently?

This same couple has a "Happy Christian Bible App" on their phone, which sends them both someone else's pre-chosen positive verse for that day; it's fast food "devotions" this verse of the day, also has someone's commentary along with it. This couple may even glance at it while they are having their "nourishing" meal, and as I compare this meal to their "spiritual food," we see a pattern. This pattern is widespread, yet it's not always seen on the surface; nor does this couple acknowledge it's a destructive pattern, because it's their way of life, the beat goes on, and they are not aware of what they are digesting. Their chosen meal is not too nourishing, and they wash it down with the worst beverage of all, diet soda. They are filled and go on with their day, thinking they are in good standing with their body (God's body) and their Spiritual health (their soul with God), but are they?

This couple, who attend a so-called "church" on Sunday, are not moved to go home and eat an organic, home-cooked meal, which means having a thorough, in-depth Bible study on what they just heard and spiritually digested at "church." They simply assume they listened to the truth and carry on with their day. Later in that day and each day of the week afterward their "App" sends it's verse, it's like having more of that diet soda, thinking they are doing their body right, thinking there's no sugar (no there's worse, there's artificial sweeteners which cause cancer) **and in that verse, while they're thinking it means one thing, it may just mean something entirely different; giving them error, a cancer of their spiritual understanding with God.** They assume, as with the diet soda, it must be okay and even good for them, not realizing its attached commentary just might have too much artificial sweetener and no salt (truth).

They have that same meal they have after "church," each day of their work week, which is all processed; the meat from that burger is from (only God knows) well, we know it's not organic, it's not grass feed and finished, it has fillers and has antibiotics; let's just look at what's in that simple, everyday fast-food meal. The way they get their deep Bible

Study is the "commentary" someone's translation from their "Happy Christian Bible App" that's the meat of their understanding, full of (only God knows). We know it's not first-hand knowledge; we know there could be someone's tradition involved in it, could be from a false teacher, could be totally wrong and even bad for them, but it's fast and that's all that matters to this couple; that's their "meat of the word", someone else's understanding of "their verse" of the day. I am not against a real hamburger (if the beef is grass-fed, no processed cheese, bun is sourdough), but fast-food burgers are full of antibiotics (feed your body sick food and you get sick, feed your mind wrong doctrine and you become a false teacher, false believer), you're eating antibiotics, fillers, hormones, and dangerous bacteria. Let's first look at the bun, it's enriched flour (bleached wheat flour, high fructose corn syrup, sugar and other ingredients like ammonium sulfate, ammonium chloride, sodium stearoyl lactylate, datem, ascorbic acid, azodicarbonamide, mono and diglycerides, ethoxylated monoglycerides, monocalcium phosphate, guar gum, calcium peroxide, soric acid, calcium propionate and/or sodium propionate (preservatives), soy lecithin) that's just the ingredients of the bun! Let's look at the ketchup: tomato concentrate, distilled vinegar, high-fructose corn syrup, corn syrup, water, salt, natural flavors (vegetable source). Since HFCS isn't enough, let's add corn syrup to the mix! Most corn is GMO. (Which alone creates massive tumors in rats) natural ingredients, including things like MSG (flavor enhancer), Aspartame (artificial sweetener), and bugs!

Let's look at the French-fries – (dextrose solution, canola oil, soybean oil, Hydrogenated soybean oil, natural beef flavor, hydrolyzed wheat, hydrolyzed milk, citric acid, dimethypolysiloxne, dextrose, sodium acid pyrophosphate salt, canola oil, corn oil, TBHQ, citric acid) this is just what's added to a potato! Then, of course, deep frying is bad in itself, which gives a higher risk of developing diseases like diabetes, heart disease, and obesity, with an increased risk of cancer thrown in; wow! Diet sodas are worse than regular sodas; the artificial sweetener used is aspartame, and diet soda also increases the risk of heart disease, strokes, obesity, kidney damage, and certain cancers. If you add cheese, you don't even want to examine the processed cheese, believe me. The point I am making here is that this couple could be you and your spouse. **Digesting false doctrine, false teaching, and you are gulping it down like it is good for you, when it just may give you a spiritual cancer.**

But this couple loves to eat out, and they never examine what they just ate or seem to care about it. Neither do they examine their "spiritual food," which is via social media or some "pastor" on Sunday. They never truly know what they are putting into their spiritual body, but they are "fat" with verses that lack true meaning and understanding. They just trust the "Happy Christian Bible App." Why wouldn't they? It's using the Bible, right? Then this couple reads the verses and their explanations through the source's commentary. Why wouldn't they believe it? It's from their "Happy Christian Bible App" from the Bible, right?

They read the verse and agree with it, even though it may have been taken out of context. Like the many verses that are misunderstood and abused by so-called "pastors" each day. For example, verses like Jeremiah 29:11 *KJV "For I know the thoughts that I think toward you, saith the Lord, thoughts of peace, and not of evil, to give you an expected end."* (Which is not what it appears, explained later) But this couple enjoys their commentary; why not? It's written by a man of "God", right? They go back again and again to that diet soda, three times a day, to read that verse, and they feel redeemed, elated, confident, even happy. Why wouldn't they? It's from their "Happy Christian Bible App," and they are walking with God, right? They give a quick word of thanks to "God" for their happy meal each day and their "Happy Christian Bible App."

The moral of this analogy is to show you that you should NOT trust your "pastor" or your "Happy Christian Bible App", or even me, for that matter. **Always examine what you read, examine what you hear, compare it to**

scripture; does it all line up? But you can't do that unless you get really deep into God's Word, which for every true Believer is a must. How can you possibly know if you are following God and doing what's right and pleasing to God, if you have no idea what is right and pleasing to God? **If you feed your Spiritual Body false teaching, false information, false understandings of verses, you are living a false "Christian life."** Then, when confronted with the Truth of God's Word, you despise it, disagree with it, and regard it as false doctrine. Well, my friend, could God look at you as a false "Christian"?

If you eat physical food each day, you should also eat Spiritual Food each day; how's your diet? If you only eat food once a week (Sunday), at best, you are malnourished and soon may die; if you study God's Word only one day a week, you are **spiritually malnourished or spiritually dead**. How would you know of false doctrine or word trickery, twisting God's Word, misinterpreting, and misunderstanding His True meanings? You won't. Only by Digging Deeper into God's Truth Defines a Christian! Again, use Expository learning and teaching, which means verse by verse, word by word, using Exegesis to draw out the exact meaning of each passage. That's really studying God's Word, seeking with your whole heart. God then gives His Children more knowledge and wisdom to discern His Word, recognize and expose false teachers, and interpret it correctly (more on this in Chapter 6).

This only happens with sincere hands-on Bible Study, not someone else's Bible Study! The time you spend in God's Word personally is vital and priceless. Write in, markup, and highlight your Bible; it's your workbook, your blueprint for your life; it is The Word of God. Keep digging and digging! A marked-up Bible is usually owned by someone whose life isn't. Be one who studies and seeks God diligently. **Ignorance of God's Word is the source of all error.** Knowledge of the Bible is the best remedy against modern heresies.

62

Let's jump over to 1 Corinthians 13:11 NKJV *When I was a child, I spoke as a child, I understood as a child, I thought as a child; but when I became a man, I put away childish things.*

Put away your childish thinking, put down that junk food diet, and start digging deeper into God's Organic Word each day. He will remove the unhealthy fillers, take away that artificial sweetener, and purify your relationship; remember, **"Digging Deeper into God's Truth Defines a Christian!"**

Regarding your physical health and well-being, give my wife's book **"God's Guide to Better Health"** a read! It's on my website.

Chapter 5: Is the Homosexual Lifestyle Accepted by God?

This is a subject of great interest today, and there is so much confusion with unbelievers and even with some believers! This goes back to chapter 2 of this book: people believing that God is so good that everything is okay with their god; he would never go against their love for another of the same sex. They say their god would love who they love, and to that I say, their god would, because their "god" doesn't exist. I hear many so-called "believers" buying into that worldly mindset, accepting such a lifestyle as okay. This is fueled by the media and liberal minded people. **The further a society drifts from the truth, the more it will hate those who declare it.** Many are afraid if they go against the main stream of the "gay lifestyle" they would be seen as an outcast; if they disagree with this wave of "gay rights" and a homosexual lifestyle and to them I say, good, you should be and feel like an outcast, a bible thumper, a radical, a fanatic because ALL true Believers are! **To be morally and biblically correct, we will go against the crowds of those who accepted this lie,** stating they were born that way, thus the need to be born again. They claim to just love, love, love, and so should you; they will go as far as calling you a hater or worse. They will say, "What would Jesus say?" Give the book, **"Many Beliefs, But God,"** a read for the answer!

Let's visit Proverbs 17:15 ESV *He who justifies the wicked and he who condemns the righteous are **both** alike an abomination to the Lord.* Here we see both those who condone, go along with, and those who commit this or any sin; God is not biased; **He hates them both equally!** If you don't say something against these sins; **if you vote a party into office that accepts such a lifestyle of sin, i.e., abortion or gay marriage, you too are as guilty as those who commit the sin.** God will not be mocked! If one celebrates, condones, parades, ignores, or in any way accepts the gay lifestyle as "normal" or "okay", or says "It's none of my business," **God says you are NOT His Child, period.**

In 1996, the Southern Baptist Convention declared concerning sexual orientation & gender identity, "Even a desire to engage in a homosexual relationship is always sinful, impure, degrading, shameful, unnatural, indecent, and perverted." We will soon see that God's Word backs up all of the above. Some think it's possible to be a **"gay Christian"; that's an oxymoron.** God will not be mocked. But first, let's look at a popular misnomer, this cliché that has come out of the modern lukewarm "church"; that we are called to love the sinner and hate the sin, let's unpack this foolish, false narrative. First of all, **God throws the sinner into Hell along with their sin.** That should be the way the statement should read, and rightfully so. God is a Righteous Judge, and therefore God hates ALL sin; that's why He sent Jesus. **Man's laws cannot make moral what God has declared immoral**; even if a sin is legalized, it's still a sin in the eyes of God. Now, to love Jesus is to obey Him and His Word; the entire Bible is His Word. Let's peek at John 14:15 KJV: *If ye love me, keep my commandments.* Jesus states the obvious, yet so many say they love Him, in word only? Let me prove that with scripture. Let's dig into Matthew 7:21-23 GNT *"Not everyone who calls me 'Lord, Lord' will enter the Kingdom of heaven, but only those who do what my Father in heaven wants them to do. When the Judgment Day comes, many will say to me, 'Lord, Lord! In your name we spoke God's message, by your name we drove out many demons and performed many miracles!' Then I will say to them, 'I never knew you. Get away from me, you wicked people!'* Here we see Jesus preaching The Sermon on the Mount. Let's dig in and unpack all this wisdom. Jesus, when He declares that NOT everyone who says, "Lord, Lord," will enter the kingdom, what does He mean? He means those who know of Him, those who even profess Him, those who were in high "church" positions, driving out demons. Those who seemingly did supernatural things in the name of Jesus. What comes to mind here are the false "churches" that profess to heal the sick, make you wealthy (if you make them wealthy first), cast out demons, repeat some prayer to be saved, name it and claim it, false religions, so many come to mind, let's keep digging. Jesus says <u>only</u> those who did the Will of His Father, as Jesus did.

Have you ever noticed that, throughout scripture, Jesus is always in constant communication with the Father? Jesus was always going off to Pray and commune with His Father. **Jesus always did the Will of His Father**. Notice Jesus is saying at Judgment Day, those who are His Elect go straight to Heaven when they die, but those who die without Jesus don't; they face Judgment Day, more on this later. <u>Jesus says to those who say they knew Him, **"I never knew you."**</u> Those are the saddest, most dejected, depressing, and miserable four words that anyone could ever hear! He calls them wicked people; in other Bible versions, evil or those who practice lawlessness; and then He sends them all into **Eternity in Hell!**

Repent and sin no more and believe Jesus is the Messiah, now die to oneself and live for Him *(this all happens simultaneously, once Born Again)*; this is the only true way out of that lifestyle. **God destroyed Sodom and Gomorrah, the reason being the homosexual lifestyles.** Father God, Jesus, and the Holy Spirit were ALL in total agreement in doing so! There was no, oh we should love, love, love them but hate their sin; **their sin is what God sees;** their sin is what sent Jesus to the cross! There were only three people whom God spared: Lot and his two daughters, as God completely destroyed those two cities. Think about this: Father God sacrificed His very own Son, allowing His slaughter, but He will let the gays slide because they are in love; not happening. Let's jump to Genesis 18:25 KJV: *That be far from thee to do after this manner, to slay the righteous with the wicked: and that the righteous should be as the wicked, that be far from thee: Shall not the Judge of all the earth do right?* Here we read that God won't misjudge anyone, but **judge them righteously, which should scare the Hell out of us all!** <u>We don't ever want His Judgment; we want His Mercy!</u>

Then there's men dressing like women, men pretending to be women, and women trying to be men. Let's go to Deuteronomy 22:5 GNT *Women are not to wear men's clothing, and men are not to wear women's clothing; the Lord your God hates people who do such things.* Cross-dressing, transvestites, multiple genders are all evil garbage, and GOD hates it! I have seen such wicked spectacles in movies and sitcoms, fools thinking it's acceptable, even funny; I assure you, my friend, God is not laughing nor will YOU be on Judgment Day, if you buy into any of it! Let's dig deeper into what God's Word says about such confused, evil, and twisted lifestyles. Let's go to Romans 1:26-27 TLB: *that is why God let go of them and let them do all these evil things, so that even their women turned against God's natural plan for them and indulged in sex sin with each other. And the men, instead of having normal sex relationships with women, burned with lust for each other, men doing shameful things with other men and, as a result, getting paid within their own souls with the penalty they so richly deserved.* When you read this, it's clear God is not accepting this lifestyle, and it's repulsive to Him; in such a way that it almost seems **He can't wait to throw them into Everlasting Torment.** If you are reading this and think this is harsh, you're not reading this with open eyes. **God is serious!**

This verse, although there are many like it, should shed light on whether God allows this. The answer is plain and evident: **NO, He detests such disgusting behavior.** That in itself doesn't mean that if you are gay, you need to stay gay. God's words are powerful, and His Grace and Mercy are available if you repent and believe. You ask what do I mean, in order to repent, you must do a 180-degree turn, meaning go the other way. Stop your lifestyle now, stop sinning, and hand your life over to Jesus Christ. And trust Him to take that behavior away permanently. **It's like this: if Jesus died for you, you now want to live for Him;** doing so, you must represent Him according to His Word, in truth. Admit you have sinned and study His Word daily for hours and hours and pray continually that He may "save" you.

cry out to Him alone, again and again…It's between You and Jesus. No one is ever responsible for your Salvation, no one. That's why Election holds true. Let me add here that Jesus died to take away our sins, past, present, and future, and He also died to give us the power to resist sin! Cry out to Him if you don't know Him, cry out! And keep crying out; **when was the last time you cried because of your sin?**

If God has truly opened your eyes, if you are one of His Elect, Born Again, you will willingly admit all your sins. You won't mis-categorize sins if God calls it an abomination, or calls something a sin, which is what God is against. And yet you still think it's okay; then you are not of The Elect, not a Child of God, or possibly a baby "Christian" at best. His Children Hear His Voice and Follow Him. Its John 14:21 ESV *"Whoever has my commandments and keeps them, he it is who loves me. And he who loves me will be loved by my Father, and I will love him and manifest myself to him."* Here, Jesus is making it known that if you truly love Him, not with just "lip service" but in your heart, you will place Him first by keeping His Commandments. Just what are these Commandments, you ask? They are ALL of His Bible; He Wrote It (it's all God breathed), so His Commandments are not limited to the 10 Commandments but all of His New Testament Teachings, as well.

Let me elaborate: let's say there is an establishment known for not agreeing with Christian Values. And they make it known (say they support abortion or gay marriage), just to give you two examples; **you should NOT support such an establishment** by purchasing their goods or using their services. I may be redundant here and elsewhere in this book for emphasis! Jesus, the Greatest Teacher of all time, was the most repetitive. Remember, the little things are as important to God as any other; **things you do and say are held for or against you, and so are the things you don't do and don't say;** God is watching. Let's visit 1 Thessalonians 5:22 KJV *Abstain from all appearance of evil.* Here we see that even the form of something wrong or bad, which you feel bad about doing, or saying, or you sense is not what God would approve of, don't do it. If you believe because the majority, or a friend, family member, or certain "pastor" says it's okay, think, what does God say in His Word about it, or to your heart, which is His and Converted, if you are His Child? **Rather than worry about who will be offended if you tell God's Truth, consider who will be misled, deceived, and destroyed if you don't.**

Deuteronomy 6:18 NKJV *And you shall do what is right and good in the sight of the Lord, that it may be well with you, and that you may go in and possess the good land of which the Lord swore to your fathers,* When Moses was appointing leaders at Sinai to help him, he gave standards to those Judges and officers he was assigning so they would in essence follow God, and practice righteous judgment. Let's go into 2 Corinthians 8:21 GNT *Our purpose is to do what is right, not only in the sight of the Lord, but also in the sight of others.* Here in Paul's second letter to the Corinthians, he finds that he has to explain the policies of giving and right thinking. He says to **do what's right in the sight of the Lord**, then what's right in the sight of others. Neither is always possible together, but remember: Paul is talking to Believers, although the Church by then had been swayed by false teachers who opposed Paul's true teachings. I am sure you will experience the same pushback if you are doing the work of God, witnessing to others, and standing up for what's right by God's Standards, even when there is strong opposition against you. **Remember God's Word is True and all others are liars.**

Christians need to make their Faith and God's correct Biblical Beliefs known; we represent God and His Kingdom. We are His Ambassadors, His Ministers, His Disciples, His Servants, His Hands and Feet, and His Mouthpiece! He placed us here to serve His Values and His Purpose, not ours. **Ask yourself, who do you represent: yourself, the world, your friends, or Jesus Christ?** Who's your daddy? He is either Satan or Father God, but in order to say you belong to God, you must be Born Again; it's never a man who tells you; you are or are not "born again," God will through His Word.

We must defend God's Word if we are His Representatives. Christians are the world's only hope toward morality, decency, respect, and right living. This reminds me of a John Calvin quote, one of my favorites. *"A dog barks when his master is attacked. I would be a coward if I saw that God's Truth is attacked and yet would remain silent."* Love it! As Christians, we need to stand up for God's Reputation and our faith 24/7 because they're being attacked on all sides, in the media, on social media, in schools, in households, and in most "churches" today as well. **Satan is busy behind many pulpits**, and he is out to confuse, steal, kill, and destroy.

John 10:6-10 NIV *Jesus used this figure of speech, but the Pharisees did not understand what he was telling them. Therefore, Jesus said again, "Very truly I tell you, I am the gate for the sheep. All who have come before me are thieves and robbers, but the sheep have not listened to them. I am the gate; whoever enters through me will be saved. They will come in and go out, and find pasture. The thief comes only to steal and kill and destroy; I have come that they may have life, and have it to the full."* Jesus is explaining, He is there to protect His Sheep (His Children) and **the thief, as in Satan, as in false teachers and those of this world, come to steal, kill, and destroy.** This also refers to the false shepherds who drew many away from the truth of the Messiah to the falsehoods of many. When Jesus says "I am," He is stating His Supreme Deity as the long-awaited Messiah. He goes on to say that if one enters through Him, they will be saved. There is no guessing here; **Jesus is proclaiming the Truth of Who He accurately is, God.**

Let's jump to Matthew 24:24 NIV *false messiahs and false prophets will appear and perform great signs and wonders to deceive, if possible, even the elect.* Here Jesus is explaining what will happen in the end times; we see this everywhere today: lies, in and out of "churches, false beliefs and false understandings, and outright falsehoods of God's Holy Word running rampant. I have even seen "churches" bring in woman pastors *(more on this later)*, gay pastors; the apostasy is outrageous and evil. Those many "church leaders" trusted in powerful positions of "ministry" leading many astray. Yet, this verse recognizes that **the Elect will not be fooled!** Amen. Notice Jesus says there will be great signs and wonders, these are not from or of Jesus; they are from the evil one. I am using these few verses to explain that just because you see a so-called "pastor" and he is gay and professes it to be okay to be gay, such is never okay with the God of the Bible, only in a "god" of their own making. Let's go To Revelation 21:8 AMP *as for the cowards and unbelieving and abominable [who are devoid of character and personal integrity and practice or tolerate immorality], and murderers, and sorcerers [with intoxicating drugs], and idolaters and occultists [who practice and teach false religions], and all the liars [who knowingly deceive and twist truth], their part will be in the lake that blazes with fire and brimstone, which is the second death."* Here is a very revealing verse into all of our final ends, our eternity. This is written so we can identify those who will inherit Heaven and those who will inherit Hell.

Let's unpack this above list: we have those called cowards, who are those who would not confess or defend Jesus, those who would turn their backs on Jesus. Then John continues with the abominable whose lifestyle is against God and His Word, those who practice the gay lifestyle, homosexuals, and those who condone or agree with such a sinful lifestyle. Murderers of innocent babies, and also those who buy into that or agree with it, those who perform sorcery, partake in horoscopes, witchcraft, Halloween, and the satanic powers of occultists. This applies to anyone who claims they can raise the dead, perform miracles, and/or speak languages known only to God. All false teachers fit into this list as well, which will fill another book. But if you understand this simple truth, that <u>God owes you nothing, we owe Him everything.</u> False gospels and counterfeit gospels like the "Prosperity gospel" or the "watered down gospel", the "gospel of love, love, love" but no repentance and no talk of sin, the "entertainment gospel", where many go to get their groove on! Remember, there are two words that should never go together, and these two words are Christian/Entertainment and Democrat/Christian, both of which are oxymorons. Christians go to Church to be fed truth and be discipled to lead others to God's Love and His Truths. When someone shows evidence of change and a sincere desire for God's Word, then they should enter a Bible-believing church. <u>Men can bring people to "church", but only The Father can bring people to Christ</u>. Please understand this: if someone brings a non-Christian into a "church," the "church" grows to accommodate the goats, not the sheep. **Biblically, no unbelievers went to "church", only Believers.** Just look at any mega "church" today, and they are filled with mostly **"make-believers."**

Read this quote from C.H. Spurgeon: *"A time will come when instead of Shepherds feeding the Sheep the church will have clowns entertaining the Goats."* Well said, Brother Charles! He was ahead of his time. I have been to "churches" where I was served coffee and popcorn before service, which I could bring into their service, and bottles of water were given out during service! I have also been to many "churches" where I had to walk out, because the message was ridiculous and totally false! Some "churches" I attended had full-blown concerts and live entertainment with dancing and singing, shows before their little sermonette; displays with smoke and laser lights; **sickening**, sickening, and sickening is the best way to describe such; others wanted money, money, and money. **They all attract the world, they attract false converts, and they attract non-Christians and give false hope to them all. Such so-called "pastors" are not saved.**

Here, Paul Washer, a Preacher and teacher, says it best! *"False teachers are God's judgment of people who don't want God but in the name of religion plan on getting everything their carnal heart desires that's why a 'Joel Osteen' is raised up, those people who sit under him are not victims of him, he is the judgment of God upon them because they want exactly what he wants **and it's not God!"*** Let's see what would support this, how about 2 Timothy 4:3-4 KJV *For the time* *will come when they will not endure sound doctrine; but after their own lusts shall they heap to themselves teachers, having itching ears; And they shall turn away their ears from the truth, and shall be turned unto fables.* Here we see a time will come (it's here now), false teachers are never challenged with God's Biblical Truths, because their doctrine is created by them, not God. But following their lusts, **false converts seek candy-coated sermons, smiling faces, or "Christian Entertainment,"** and, as false believers, "make believers" go where they feel comfortable, blend in, or are never offended because of their personal sins, and biblical correction does not exist. When these fake "Christians" do this, they begin to believe multiple varieties of nonsense and worldly garbage, which is in total opposition to God's Word. Even rebellious fake believers are part of God's Sovereign Will. He can use their seeking after "feel good" sermons, then drop them to their knees, after a real Christian confronts their foolishness with God's Truths. **Be that REAL Christian; speak Bold Truth into someone's life.** Sometimes you may have to "point a finger" in their face and say NO! **Pointing a finger, even if in a rhetorical imaginary pointing gesture, reprimands someone, stopping them in their tracks** to think, pray, and study God's Word *(if this person is a true Believer),* change will happen.

Now, if you truly feel the passion (possibly because you were personally caught up in that same error), pointing a finger is spontaneous, challenging, intimidating, and such a visual carries power, attracting the listener's full attention. Whichever you decide to do, led by The Holy Spirit, remember you only do this because you love the Truth and love the person you are rebuking. Start with 2 Timothy 3:16 to provide a foundation for correction. Be prepared to answer all questions on any subject matter. Remember, you should always defend God's Truths and His Word daily; this is why **studying His Word is imperative**, it's 2 Timothy 4:2 NKJV *Preach the word! Be ready in season and out of season. Convince, rebuke, exhort, with all longsuffering and teaching.* Christians should always look forward to preaching and teaching the lost and rebuking, if necessary, especially if they are unlearned baby Christians or falsely taught Christians by false teachers. **All true Believers love to be corrected and get God's Word right.** Those who fight God's Scripture once the Truth of Scripture is shown and explained are of the world; it's easy to spot the lost (false convert): they will argue against **God's Truths, not agree with them.**

God can reverse the lost so they are desperately seeking His Truth. It's happened to me; years before I was saved, I attended a Pentecostal "church" for about a year. The time came when I felt I should join the "church" as a member, so I attended their membership class and filled out the paperwork. There was a question about whether I spoke in tongues. I answered no, so the "pastor" read that on my paperwork and called me to ask if I was ready to learn tongues. I replied, "I thought it was a gift from God?" He then said, "we teach it here, you would have to repeat after me, then mix up some of these words I use and add some of your own," so I laughed (remember I was not Born Again, yet I was smart enough to see through their nonsense) I asked, "if you can give out gifts, I rather the gift of NBA Basketball player, can you give me that one?" He was shocked and speechless, and I left that foolish so-called "church". You see, even as an unsaved person, **I still had common sense.** Thinking back, I didn't realize anyone else there was "saved" because they thought I was, and we were all seemingly lost, a dead church. We were the blind leading the blind. There was no accountability, no transformation, no change of heart, no spiritual rebirth, no regeneration, no sanctification, no nothing, just jumping up and down with their silly music and claiming victory over everything and everybody; **all complete nonsense and such a deceptive bunch,** but the "pastor" was a funny guy. His jokes and personality kept me coming back, **because I was NOT SAVED!** Now I see clearly, not through a dark lens, and would only attend such a "church" for research purposes, because I write Christian Poetry and Christian Books. And writing about false teachers is important for Believers to identify, expose, and remove them from their lives.

Thinking about that now, I feel so stupid and ashamed. I was tricked into thinking I was "saved" and that the "church" had correct doctrine and would teach me God's Truths. This, and many other reasons, is why each of us must read and study the Bible on our own before finding a "church." How would you know if you're getting bamboozled into a false teaching "church" or an entertainment-type "church" with jokes and erroneous teachings? Pentecostal "churches" are based on the twisting of God's Word. Their dogma is based on a "name it and claim it" mentality; **it's all about money, the pride of life, getting all you want, which is everything Satan offers.** They buy into a "prosperity gospel," which is the gospel of lies. The charismatic movement (charismania) takes the uneducated "church goers" and teaches them how to misuse the Biblical Scriptures. Therefore, controlling and molding their minds so they are convinced they deserve whatever they want, and that their god is their Santa Claus, their genie in a bottle; they seek only "gifts," not the Giver.

They lack discernment of God's Word. In most cases, the spirit in them is not of "God" but of satanic powers or of their own foolish selves, human depravity, and an unconverted heart. Once one of their parishioners' eyes is opened by God to that evil cult, they flee from it. Yes, God may lead some out of that brainwashing, false-teaching cult. God does this to show His Power. Once one is Born Again, they leave that denomination quickly and rejoice in the fact that God showed them His True Mercy and Grace. I was one to whom God showed His extreme love. We all deserve Hell, but for God, His Mercy, and His Grace. Matthew 16:24-25 NKJV: *Then Jesus said to His disciples, "If anyone desires to come after Me, let him deny himself, and take up his cross, and follow Me. For whoever desires to save his life will lose it, but whoever loses his life for My sake will find it.* We see the qualifications to follow Jesus, which are that we deny ourselves. This is only done by placing Christ first in our lives, before ourselves, before family, and before friends. It's living for Him and only Him. **If Jesus is not in control of your life, your life still belongs to you.**

As far as finding a "church," seek one that is Bible-based. I always recommend a **Reformed** Baptist Church. Test the Spirits to be certain they are of the same Spirit. It's 1 John 4:1 MSG: *My dear friends, don't believe everything you hear. Carefully weigh and examine what people tell you. Not everyone who talks about God comes from God. **There are a lot of lying preachers loose in the world.*** Here, John is making us aware of what's happening in most churches, and today. I will add that Televangelists, Radio Talk Shows, and most sermons, along with the majority of books out there, are false and lies from the Evil One (Satan). How would you know, you ask? Well, if a "pastor" says **"repeat after me"** nonsense, and "you're saved," if you make his prayer your prayer, then says, "welcome to the family," that's one to watch out for, because only God makes Christians, and God's Word will let you know if and when you are saved or not saved. **Refer to point #1.** As for other sure signs of false teachers, some tell you to tithe. The tithe is an Old Testament law that never applies to blood-bought Christians; more on that later. Another sign of false teachers is that they want your money and make you feel guilty if you question their motives. Some false teachers use these lines. Once they get you to recite their own prayer and make it yours, they'll say, *"Your name was just now written in the Book of Life!"* This is yet **another lie;** all of The Elect's names were written in the **Book of Life before the foundation of the world**; that was when God chose them and gave them to the Lord Jesus to save and own.

Let's dig into Revelation 17:8 NLT: *The beast you saw was once alive but isn't now. And yet he will soon come up out of the bottomless pit and go to eternal destruction. And the people who belong to this world, whose names were not written in the Book of Life before the world was made, will be amazed at the reappearance of this beast who had died.* Let's unpack this verse. An angel is interpreting the mystery of

John's vision. The beast is the Antichrist, who deceives the world through his false "resurrection." The bottomless pit is Hell, his final destination. The people of the world are those here when this happens. The key reason I went to this book at all is to prove that when the Book of Life was written, it was written **before time began**, before the foundation of the world. So, when you hear the next false teacher tell someone their name was just written in the "Book of Life." Now, you know **they are false teachers,** doing their thing and being deceitful. Some even say "come get saved" or "get your miracle here," and use other carnival tactics. Throughout this book, I often go off topic, but to make a Biblical point, I have to. Because the Bible will defend itself and it's all tied together, such is God's Truth. Give the book, **"Examine The End Times,"** a read, because you should know what's coming.

Let's get back to Leviticus 18:22 KJV *Thou shalt not lie with mankind, as with womankind: it is an abomination.* Leviticus 20:13 KJV *If a man also lie with mankind, as he lieth with a woman, both of them have committed an abomination: they shall surely be put to death; their blood shall be upon them.* Here we clearly read that God is so against man with man and woman with woman, He Says They Shall be put to Death. **God says it's an abomination**, meaning a thing that causes Him **Great Disgust;** it's an atrocity, an evil outrage to God. Jump now to Jude 1:7 NLT *and don't forget **Sodom and Gomorrah** and their neighboring towns, which were filled with immorality and every kind of sexual perversion. Those cities were destroyed by fire and serve as a warning of the eternal fire of God's judgment.*

As we see clearly in God's Word, there is no escaping God's judgment for such a lifestyle; and there is no such thing as "gay pride", that is an oxymoron. **God the Father, Jesus, and the Holy Spirit were all in total agreement to kill everyone in those two cities because of their lifestyles of sin.** Yes, they are all Hellbound! What young people are taught today in many "churches" is that Jesus is so loving; He will take you as you are and leave you thinking "don't worry," just come as you are, and I will love you anyway; such twisting and false thinking of today's baby "Christian." Jesus will always take His Children the way they are. But He NEVER leaves them to themselves. He Changes Their Hearts to be and think as His Word teaches, and ALL of His Children Obey, not just some. Believers fully acknowledge that the Bible is right and they are wrong. Go now to Romans 1:25-27 ESV *because they exchanged the truth about God for a lie and worshiped and served the creature rather than the Creator, who is blessed forever! Amen. For this reason God gave them up to dishonorable passions. For their women exchanged natural relations for those that are contrary to nature; and the men likewise gave up natural relations with women and were consumed with passion for one another, men committing shameless acts with men and receiving in themselves the due penalty for their error.* God is clear here as well, rejecting God and His standards; eventually, God removes any restraints and allows their sin to run rampant, **left to their own demise.** God allows them to fulfill their desires because soon He will cast them **into Hell**, where they will spend Eternity. As for false books, written by false teachers about how the "gay life" is "Christian" or that "woman pastors" are "Christian," these usually have the writer's face on it bigger than the book's title! Think about this, why would a "pastor" want fame when God promises His Children Glory? **The Christian life is not about self-promotion; it's about self-denial.** Don't buy into making these so-called "pastors" who are frauds, rich or richer, or any more popular, but **expose them for the charlatans they are.** You can't buy God's blessings, so don't purchase their books; **it's deceitful hype**. John MacArthur said, *"Satan is most effective in the church when he comes not as an open enemy, not as a false friend; not when he attacks the pulpit, but **when he stands in it!"*** This is a true statement; I have witnessed this many times! This statement is clear, and it should also trouble you, especially if you don't even know HOW to identify a false teacher. Hopefully, after this book, you will, God willing! Let's keep digging...

Chapter 6: Does God Promise a Better Life if You Choose to Follow Him?

If by now <u>you have noticed this question itself is fundamentally flawed,</u> **congratulations**, you are focusing on what you are reading! Amen. Of course, no one can choose to follow Him; it's He that does ALL the Choosing, John 15:16-19 NKJV *You did not choose Me, but I chose you and appointed you that you should go and bear fruit, and that your fruit should remain, that whatever you ask the Father in My name He may give you. These things I command you, that you love one another. "If the world hates you, you know that it hated Me before it hated you. If you were of the world, the world would love its own. Yet because you are not of the world, but I chose you out of the world, therefore the world hates you.* Let's unpack these four verses. Jesus is explaining that no one chooses Him; He did ALL of the Salvational Choosing as far as being of the Elect is concerned, as we know from chapter one. **There is no such thing as "free will" for Salvation; it's all God's Will.** And Jesus continues to explain that we are selected to bear fruit. What He is saying is that all Believers will bear fruit (lead some to Him and teach others His Truths), asking only in His Father's name what is in God's Will, not ours. So many misunderstand this verse as well, it's not about cars, homes, money, it's ALL about doing His Father's Will. He says to love one another. This is a good sign of an unbeliever; if he or she harbors hate for someone else, they are not His children. **Yet we are to hate what God hates and love what God loves.** It's not confusing; if we are Christians, we are to correct others. Many ask me, *"What's God's Will for my life?"* I tell them, *"It's to study God's Word and Obey it!"* Let's look again at 2 Timothy 3:16 KJV *All scripture is given by inspiration of God, and is profitable for doctrine, for reproof, for correction, for instruction in righteousness:* This scripture is so important to me, it was painted across my living room wall. Now in my new home, it's on my kitchen wall! This verse should be vitally important in each Christian's life. **I love biblical correction, and so should you!**

The reason why this verse is so important is that we all make mistakes, **we all need correction, rebuke, and God's Word will do that;** and those who know you should rebuke you when you are wrong. They should **keep you accountable to God.** When I was a new Christian, baby Christian years ago, although I studied God's Word 2 to 5 hours each day, once I was saved, I listened to about 35 sermons each week, for years, did not watch ANY TV for 6 years. Yet, I was still a baby Christian in deep error for the first two years of my Salvation! I once told a mentor of mine that I deserved to be wealthy, that I was a Child of The King! What happened next still stirs me up to study more and more; I am always seeking more Truths in God's Word each day. My friend snapped at me, **pointing his finger, saying, "No, You Don't!"** Well, I was not going to challenge him like many unlearned believers do today. I said nothing, but started a 3-month study on just the "prosperity gospel". While studying this subject, I listened to countless false teachers, read their deceptive books, and tried to align their words with God's, until I reached a point where I could see and grasp the truth. I was previously brainwashed. While young, I attended a Catholic "church," then a Baptist "church," then a Pentecostal "church," and non-denominational "churches" as well, all before I was saved; all that nonsense, **cult teachings**, lies, and false teaching rubbed off. So, at the conclusion of my endeavor to seek all areas and dig deep into God's Word, I was unequivocally wrong! I had to **relearn the Bible** through the eyes of One Born Again, with The Help of the Holy Spirit. **The Scriptures illuminated, and I saw truths I had never seen before!** I went back and told my friend you were correct: God owes me nothing, and I owe Him everything. Thank you for the rebuke! He was happy, because I spent much time alone with God's Word and God Opened My Eyes even more to His Truths, as He Still Does Each and Every Day!

Let me tell you about an eye-opening true event. Years ago, I had a long walk with a woman who told me she was a "pastor" and spoke "tongues"; I told her NO to both and that she was seriously mistaken. I told her the apostolic age is over and cited scripture. I started in 1 Corinthians 13:8 KJV *Charity never faileth: but whether there be prophecies, they shall fail; whether there be tongues, they shall **cease**; whether there be knowledge, it shall vanish away.* I talked to her for hours about these matters; I explained that the word "cease" meant STOP permanently, and that tongues had ended when the last Apostle, John, died on the island of Patmos. Tongues were a sign to the unbeliever that the person using tongues was from God because it was their own language that the other person heard. Tongues were always learned languages and were always used to explain the Gospel. If this gift were still real and active today, missionaries would not have to take two years of language study in the area they travel to; they would use those with that gift. Well, she was not convinced; **facts and Biblical Truths will not convince those who are not willing to study and allow God's Word to penetrate their Hearts and minds.** Even some Elect find it hard to accept the change to God's Truths because of their traditions and their leaning on their own past understanding. Most won't at first cling to all of God's Truths, mainly because they bought into believing false teachers and their lies. Remember, even some of God's Children need to learn the hard way. Like when I thought the "prosperity gospel" was true. You see, God's Children Will Seek His Truths; God will use many others to humble and enlighten His Own Children. He doesn't want His Children in the dark because We are His Light!

That's why I wrote this book, it's John 21:15-17 NKJV *So when they had eaten breakfast, Jesus said to Simon Peter, "Simon, son of Jonah, do you love Me more than these?" He said to Him, "Yes, Lord; You know that I love You." He said to him, "Feed My lambs." He said to him again a second time, "Simon, son of Jonah, do you love Me?" He said to Him, "Yes, Lord; You know that I love You." He said to him, "Tend My sheep." He said to him the third time, "Simon, son of Jonah, do you love Me?" Peter was grieved because He said to him the third time, "Do you love Me?" And he said to Him, "Lord,*

You know all things; You know that I love You." Jesus said to him, "Feed My sheep". Here we see Jesus asking Peter, who had denied Him three times, whether he loved Him more than those around Him; the question was eye-opening. Now note the answer. The lesson from Jesus: first, He said, *"Feed My Lambs," which are baby Sheep or newly Born Believers (under 2 years saved).* Then Jesus asks again to Peter *"Do you love me?"* Peter replies, *"Yes Lord You know that I love You,"* here we see a pattern, a message from The Master Teacher Himself; Jesus then says, *"Tend My Sheep"* Here we see Jesus instruct Peter and Us to first teach the New Believers (feed milk), then help them grow in Truth; (continue teaching them). Then Jesus asks Peter a third time, *"Do you love Me?"* Peter replies, *"Lord you know all things, you know that I love you."* Jesus said, *"Feed My Sheep,"* here Jesus is putting the nail in the coffin, He is clear and specific in what **He wants and what He Commands from all Believers today.** Note the pattern, feed the babies in Christ (baby food), unlearned Believers, guide them by tending to them (follow up), and finally feed The Sheep, **teach with clarity the meat of The Word,** dig and go deep into it, sanctification. The True Word of God, and this cycle is repeated from generation to generation, which brings us to this very day. **Are you discipling others, feeding God's Truths to others, or are you confused as to what Truth is?**

Back to my story: after a few hours had passed, as I thoroughly explained God's Truths to that lady, she said she never wanted to see me again. You will notice that few will ever confront others in the same "faith" as being wrong. **Most people don't really want the Truth anyway; they just want constant reassurance that what they believe is the truth.** But this lady had my phone number, and, remarkably, about 6 months later, **she called me** to ask if I remembered her. I said, *"Yes, I did,"* she went on to tell me I was right; she was no longer, nor was she ever really a woman pastor because **women could never be pastors**, and I agreed. It's 1 Timothy 2:11-13 KJV *Let a woman learn in silence with all submission. And I do not permit a woman to* *teach or to have authority over a man, but to be in silence. For Adam was formed first, then Eve.* She went on to quote Titus 1:6 GNT: *"An elder must be without fault; he must have only one wife, and his children must be believers and not have the reputation of being wild or disobedient."* Here we see that a woman cannot even become an elder of any "church", unless it's a "church" that is dead (Godless). These verses and more were the very same verses I spent time explaining to her. And now she was <u>reading them back to me</u> over the phone! **How is this possible, you ask?** This was a sign of a True Child of God, **one who would take the rebuke and correction another gives them and then line it up with scripture** and not the fables and misinterpretations of men. Back when we met, she was confused and misled down the road where all false teachers live; unless derailed by another more seasoned Christian able to help guide that person to God's Truths, debunking and exposing the lies taught by false religions and so-called "Christian" pastors. Many would go through their whole life, living a lie – Jesus said many times to others, *"Haven't YOU read?"* God's Truths are vital and without them shows a detachment to Him, a lack of Bible Study, a cavalier attitude, and an unregenerate heart, which is equivalent to a false convert, a lost soul.

Then this lady said, *"I really cannot speak in tongues because no one today can,"* she was pleased and thanked me for giving her **the cold, hard Truth.** I said, *"You're welcome, and God did ALL the work in your heart, Amen!"* God works through His Children, which is a privilege, but in His Time, not ours. We must always speak the Truth in love, and if that seems impossible, then be like John the Baptist and yell it! **Point your finger at them and say NO!** Thank God for 2 Timothy 3:16, and if this happens to you in any area of questioning, it's God's Way of saying study! Visit with me for the second time to 2 Timothy 2:15 KJV *Study to shew thyself approved unto God, a workman that needeth not to be ashamed, rightly dividing the word of truth.* Again, God wants you to take His Word seriously, in truth. Studying is vital. **Getting His Word right is not going to fly well with false**

teachers, false converts, and this fallen world, but you MUST be a proponent of Truth, speaking and living God's Truths to Glorify God. A Christian may be in serious doctrinal errors; typically, "baby Christians" and this should last only a short time **(under 2 years), and you should have read through the whole bible by then.** If the Holy Spirit is in you, your seeking of God's Truth will lead you to study His Word more deeply, or guide you to a simple book like this, but if you think about it, **this book has well over 300 Bible verses in it!** When my friend and mentor pointed his finger at me, saying NO you don't believe the 'prosperity gospel,' you don't believe that! When I thought I deserved riches, I would have therefore continued in my error. **If I didn't tell this lady God's Truths and point at her, saying NO, the Apostolic era is over;** you do not know tongues, and you are not a Pastor! Then she may have gone on, in error, for decades, or for her lifetime. If you surround yourself with other false believers, you need to hear from God through a Real Believer. Let me ask YOU, **who is pointing a finger at you today and saying NO!** Be bold in Truth, God sees all, or do you need to point your finger at a loved one or a fellow Christian today? **Or is this book pointing a finger at YOU?**

I want to explain now how to read and interpret God's Word accurately. **Expository Preaching** and teaching means verse by verse; this is how the Bible should be taught. But from my experience in "church" attendance countless times and especially at every **Arminian-type "church" (a liberal movement of false Christianity, started by Jacob Arminius in the 17ᵗʰ century),** the "pastor" stops reading right before any "Chosen or Elected" verse because such a verse would explain and reveal God's Election. **This is because being an Arminian (freewill salvationist)** doesn't actually believe the whole bible, just the text they expound on. **Either you believe ALL of what the Bible says or none of it; there is no in-between! Like, there's no such thing as being half pregnant!** Let me further explain using Biblical **Exegesis**, which means interpreting the text based on careful, objective analysis. The word "exegesis " means to "draw out" to "get from", **allowing the text to speak for itself**. This is what's best, of course. It's using observation; what is this passage saying, who is it talking to, referring to, what does it imply, what does this passage mean, and how does it relate to the rest of the Bible, and finally, how does it relate to my life today? This is the correct view on how we can grow in our Faith and His Truths, which are not taught in most "churches." But you can start reading, studying the Bible, and growing from this day forth correctly. **True unity in Christ is only built upon sound Doctrine and Correct Theology.** Attending a "Seminary or Christian College" is **no** guarantee that you will learn God's Word correctly; you may even be taught erroneous teaching. **Many well-known FALSE TEACHERS went to a "Seminary".** There are many "faith movements" that communicate unbiblical teaching, distorting Biblical concepts of faith, taught by false converts. There are also many Arminian "Colleges and Seminaries" and even those that teach Pentecostalism! Beware: these are all False Doctrines, and they are the "teachings" you must avoid! I find **The Master's Seminary to be one of the best.** Remember, many "teachers" themselves are not even "saved" and are teaching the Bible. A man not "saved" cannot accurately teach God's Word, period. You cannot be taught by a school that misinterprets Scripture, or one that has its own understanding of Scripture, or misunderstanding; remember, there are over 60 "Christian" denominations. Charles Spurgeon had no formal education, yet was known as the "Prince of Preachers." Beware, some seminaries will place you on the false teachers list! Choose wisely if you go that route; never allow others to "teach" you what the Bible doesn't; and **always use Biblical Exegesis!** John 16:14 (AMP) *He will glorify and honor Me, (Jesus) because He (the Holy Spirit) will take from what is Mine and will disclose it to you.* The Holy Spirit will never go against the Bible and will always exalt The Lord Jesus Christ; each Believer is given The Holy Spirit, the very second one is Born Again.

Okay, then, there's **Eisegesis**, which is the opposite approach to deciphering scripture. So many so-called "pastors" use this **false interpretation** of God's Word in a biased way, and they have their own agendas in doing so. Many mishandle scripture to gain your money, such as tithing, more on that one later. Using **Eisegesis**, one would approach scripture and interpret it through a subjective, non-analytical reading. It's someone injecting their own meaning or opinion into the text **(a tactic used by false teachers).** They make the text mean what they want it to mean, misinterpret it, then try to support it, taking yet other verses out of context, and butchering them as well. It's the mishandling of the text in a misleading way, which applies imagination; whatever idea the "preacher" is creating or presenting that day. It's a way of twisting verses and text to fit their story. Reading into the text whatever the writer or "preacher" wants, which is a false narrative, and this is, of course, against God. As we see, simply identifying such preachers and writers using Exegesis (explain & interpret) and expository learning (verse by verse) will eliminate most false teachers from your future hearing and reading choices. Then there's **Hermeneutics**, which means interpretation. When preaching or teaching the Bible, we interpret and translate the text and pursue its real meaning. **Applying Exegesis to what we read is, in itself, a form of Hermeneutics: taking into account the original language and its history, and using Scripture to interpret Scripture.**

C.H. Spurgeon was quoted as saying, *"Visit many good books, but live in the Bible."* Remember the Bible interprets the Bible. I attended an Arminian "church"; for many years, even after being saved, such "church" goers believe that one could choose God at any time and un-choose Him as well. A person who believes they can choose Jesus one day, also believes they can choose another "god" on a different day. Think of this, let's say you "accept" Jesus; you say a prayer some "pastor" led you in. Well, that day, you think you are "saved" as you would believe, on your way to Heaven. So, if you died that day, you would certainly feel you were Heaven-bound. **Let's say a week later, you now choose the Islamic**

faith, you now feel that Muhammad is who you should follow, and of course, in doing so, you denounce Jesus as God, as Savior. And let's say you die that week, and so you are now Hell-bound, but only if you died a week earlier while you believed Jesus was The Only Way to Heaven, you would have spent eternity with Jesus? **Are you beginning to see how foolish the Arminian thinking is?** It's not Bible-based; it's a false belief pattern that divides the Tares from the Wheat or the Sheep from the goats (unconverted, the unregenerate heart), sees things without the help of the Holy Spirit, which only God's Elect would have. No one can truly rescue themselves from God's Wrath, or come to Jesus on their own terms or at their own timing. **Biblically, only a boastful person would ever, ever argue that he or she is the captain of his or her own soul; such a belief comes from a false understanding of scripture.** We know from our study in Chapter 1 that it is never the case. Although I knew this for years while attending an Arminian "church," my going there was based on the fact that so few "churches" even use a Bible today. The "church" I attended did; they even gave Bibles to those who did not own one. Choosing the right "church" is a process of elimination; a sad truth. But did you notice something I said in the last few sentences? If so, you are awakened by God. If someone attending a "church" today doesn't own a Bible (In America), this more than likely shows they are unbelievers; unbelievers shouldn't be brought to "church" to "get saved". Again, Christians who bring unbelievers to their "church" should first witness to them, give them the Gospel, and lead them in truth to the Lord. If that person is receptive and God opens their eyes to His Truths, great, **then bring them.**

The reason being, in the Bible, gatherings were with and for **only Believers, not unbelievers.** What unbeliever wants to be fed God's Truths before he or she is "Born Again", his stomach can't bear it? Such a person can grow hardened and confused before God opens their eyes, if God ever will. This is why Christians everywhere are called to give the Gospel to whom they meet and are led by the Holy Spirit to do so. **Every SAVED person is a Missionary; every UNSAVED person is the mission field.** We Are All Ministers of the Word of God! The field is ready for harvest. Today, we see "pastors" encouraging their flock to bring in their friends and neighbors, because "church" growth in these types of "churches" is not real church growth. There are so few of The Elect, the Sheep, who attend such "churches," and they leave when they are not truly fed. It's the goats that fill the pews, and the "pastor" accommodates the goats (lost) and starts **entertaining them to keep them coming back**. This "pastor" will have jokes and a winning personality. Then they try their alter call "gimmick" or "raise your hand" tactic, both of which are unbiblical and cause more harm than good. I was a participant in that nonsense, and it confused many, many years of my life. As I said earlier in Chapter 1, I felt I had "fire insurance", since I walked an aisle, said some words, even got baptized, reciting someone's prayer and making it yours, is against God's Word and **not found anywhere in scripture.**

Examine yourself, it's 2 Corinthians 13:5 AMP: *Test and evaluate yourselves to see whether you are in the faith and living your lives as [committed] believers. Examine yourselves! Or do you not recognize this about yourselves [by an ongoing experience] that Jesus Christ is in you—unless indeed you fail the test and are rejected as counterfeit?* Here, in the second letter to the Corinthians, Paul issues a very serious warning: he rings a bell, delivering a reality check! **He points a finger!** Paul says **EXAMINE YOURSELVES!** He asked, are you a committed Believer, or on the fence (in other words), if you are not ALL in, banking 100% on Jesus, trusting Him with your whole life; Paul says you are a counterfeit, or other translations say a reprobate (dammed to Hell). We must all examine ourselves. John MacArthur was quoted as saying, *"If the demons believe, tremble, and are not saved, what does that say about those who profess to believe and don't even tremble?"*

And since getting saved (Born Again) through the Grace of God, my eyes have witnessed "pastors" using "used

DIGGING DEEPER INTO GOD'S TRUTH DEFINES A "CHRISTIAN"   JOSEPH MALARA

car salesman techniques" **to guilt many to walk that aisle,** say this prayer, or that prayer; I would get up and leave the building at that time. **Such a display angers God; it does not please Him. It's smacking God in the face** when these "pastors" take "Salvation" into their own hands, taking away from God's Glory. God will never share His Glory with these false teachers or anyone, for that matter. I have witnessed "pastors" say, "Come on down," or "You tried everything else, now try Jesus." Just typing this makes me nauseous. How do you think God feels? They say, "It's so easy even cavemen can do it." **NO, it's so hard ONLY God can do it!** False teaching is everywhere today, and these so-called "pastors" boast of how many they got to walk that isle (how many they "saved," or baptized). It's appalling. Note the small "s"; people are not numbers. I assure you, God is not impressed.

I hear many say they must persuade others of God's Word, **convince them of the Gospel, what a disgrace; as if God needs those so-called** "pastors" boasting of their powers to influence, their **skills at manipulation**, and their ability to pass guilt on many to gain more converts. That leads only to **false converts** who embrace a watered-down "feel-good" gospel or a "motivational" gospel. Which in turn leads to "fake Christians" who were coerced and bamboozled into believing, and then there are those "pastors" using logic or "Christian Apologetics" (defending Christianity by giving objective reasons and evidence that Christianity is true) to convince many, **as if facts about The Bible matter to the lost? They don't, they're dead, they're blind, unless God awakens (quickens) them.** All an unbeliever needs is the Gospel over and over, **baby food, only baby food**. With only facts, we end up getting well-informed unbelievers who are able to "somewhat" even teach the Bible, **yet are not themselves saved.** They become *Arminian* at best, believing only most of the Bible and misunderstanding the rest. **An agnostic, a heathen, or an infidel may also intellectually accept many Gospel facts.** But without a **miracle** from God to open his or her eyes, convert a heart, to transform a mind, to wake up a dead soul, this person is but a mere

89

theologically informed pagan and NOT a Christian. A.W. Tozer said, *"Many people say, Try Jesus."* You don't "Try" Jesus. He's not there to be experimented with. **Christ is NOT on trial – you are!**

The choice for Salvation is 100% God and 0% us; no one can make one believe all of God's Word or The Gospel of Jesus Christ but God, when and if God is ready to do so. **What these blind leaders do is lead other blind people down a path of choosing**, as to what to believe in as far as God's Word; **a smorgasbord religion, one where the "pastor" cherry-picks** what Jesus can do for you, your marriage, your bills, your health, and says choose Jesus and get all this thrown in! **No, Jesus alone is worthy.** Jesus with more personal grief, Jesus with more financial woes, Jesus with more personal pain is well worth it. **What I never see from "pastors" today is a real comparison to the lives of the Apostles themselves; compared to most Christians' lives today, maybe then we can have a true perspective of biblical reality!**

Many "pastors" today use Eisegesis to twist God's true meanings of verses they can't explain or won't; it's false teaching 101, you must be cautious of this. This way of false teaching is thriving throughout Christianity today. And it totally takes away God's Glory, and we are warned about this many times in scripture; let's go to Luke 6:26 NLT *What sorrow awaits you **who are praised by the crowds, for their ancestors also praised false prophets***. What comes to your mind here, or who comes to your mind; have you ever witnessed clapping in any "church"? Have you ever experienced "celebrity pastors" being praised by non-believers, some even worshipped? That's what Jesus is saying here. **Do you have many non-believers who speak well of you? If they hated Jesus, they will hate you as well. If not, maybe you are not representing Jesus but representing yourself.** As a Christian, life is not a popularity contest, but a life dead to oneself and <u>alive only to and for and in Jesus the Christ.</u> **It's ALL about Him and not us.** Paul said it best from within prison walls. Let's dig into

Philippians 1:21 KJV *For to me to live is Christ, and to die is gain.* Here, Paul, in prison, is saying that for him to live is all Christ. Telling all others about Jesus and what He has done for Paul. Telling all others about the Salvation that is only in Jesus, the long-awaited Messiah, the Christ! For Paul to die is ALL gain! Yes, Heaven was waiting for Paul. He was content to know His Savior and the Truth; are you?

R. C. Sproul, an American theologian, said it this way: *"The greatest weakness in the church today is that the servants of God keep looking over their shoulder for the approval of man."* Most Christians today are catering to the lost, not feeding The Sheep. Therefore, the "churches" that think they can personally convert the lost and they can't, only do an injustice to God's Children who suffer under such foolish leadership. These "churches" are merely a revolving door of the few Elect and the many lost. There is no foundation, no substance, and little accountability from behind the pulpit. The false teachers in these so-called "churches" seldom speak about **Sin**, **Repentance**, or **Hell**. These "churches" are baby "churches," they only try to feed the lambs, and keep each parishioner a lamb, because they don't get into God's Word to DIG deep. This brings me to another point of interest: most lost "churches" don't use a pulpit; they use a "cool look," walking back and forth, telling stories with few Bible verses or just choice ones. No deep study of the Word; some use cartoons (I have witnessed this), and others use video clips of their own so-called achievements, which is vanity. I even witnessed one "pastor" wearing his leather jacket, even though it was 90 degrees outside, as some sort of gimmick, style, or trademark. Some "churches" have full-blown concerts with smoke and laser lights! **It's "Showtime" in false "churches" today! God is certainly not pleased with such nonsense; He is not present at all in such congregations in front of or behind their pulpit, if they even have one.**

What happens to the few Sheep in such congregations, you ask? They stay for a while and are never truly fed; they then become weary, confused, and upset because they are of the Elect, thirsty for God's Word. They leave, find another church, become "churchless," watch a live online service from gty.org, or approach that pastor with Biblical Truths. But, as my experience has shown, these so-called "pastors" are only concerned with their traditions and larger congregations, and change is rare, if at all. They want larger buildings, adding to what they have financially and in personal status; greed. Some own private jets, several houses, and make huge, huge salaries, own yachts, and have fans that love them, buy their books, and adore them! Remember, all the Apostles but one were murdered; they all had nothing but God's Truths. **Jesus had no place to lay His Head;** true alliance to Jesus is to serve others, not rob them blind!

There was a year when I was attending a "church," and two separate Bible studies a week; one at a different church, another at a brother's house. The one at a "church" building comprised of 20 men; most attended that "church" where the Bible study was held. By the end of that year, none of them were attending that "church" any longer, because it was an "entertainment church". And when one is fed Truth, discipled in and by The True Word of GOD, a Born-Again Christian can't continue in false teachings of any kind, or foolishness for long. Let's move over to Luke 9:57-62 NKJV *now it happened as they journeyed on the road, that someone said to Him, "Lord, I will follow You wherever You go." And Jesus said to him, "Foxes have holes and birds of the air have nests, but the* **Son of Man has nowhere to lay His head.** *Then He said to another, "Follow Me." But he said, "Lord, let me first go and bury my father." Jesus said to him,* **"Let the dead bury their own dead,** *but you go and preach the kingdom of God." And another also said, "Lord, I will follow You, but let me first go and bid them farewell who are at my house." But Jesus said to him, "No one, having put his hand to the plow, and looking back, is fit for the kingdom of God."* Let's unpack these six verses; they're much more telling than they may appear. Jesus is confronted with many men, but not true followers, just halfhearted, friendly men. Jesus explains that He has no home, no place to lay His Head, and that this was His reality. Jesus showing us that only His Elect Will ever Follow Him; let me further explain; Jesus says to a man "Follow Me", the man gives an excuse to bury his dad, (this was a common figure of speech meaning he wanted to wait until his dad died for inheritance) then Jesus says *"Let the dead bury the dead,"* wow, Jesus was saying they were dead in Him as well, **let the dead bury the dead;** remember Jesus is God and knows all things and therefore He knows who are His and who are not, nor ever will be. He teaches them in a way they can relate to; Jesus says that if one is plowing a field and turns to look back, he will not plow straight, and if one follows Jesus, they must be all in to follow Him. Few "Christians" today are all in, and few "churches" have "pastors" who are Born Again Believers willing to risk telling the Truth of God's Word, regardless of what many are told; these above verses show that **any Arminian view of God's Word is a Satanic lie.**

The Arminian view would be that we decide and provide the significant faith in ourselves, without God. But the Biblical view is that we cannot, in and of ourselves, choose to have enough faith to glorify God or make ourselves a true Believer, in other words, make ourselves The Elect. To differentiate between someone who believes in Arminianism, or Biblical Truths, which is the meaning of Calvinism you can simply ask him or her; this person who declares they are a "Christian" simply ask them, *"What was the decisive reason for your faith in Christ?"* and listen to their answer, was it all God or in part their decision? Did that person pick God by saying a prayer, asking God to save them, or saying they accepted Jesus, chose Him, invited Him, or received Him by asking? Or did they think Jesus was a gentleman and would never push His way in? **I have heard them all,** even a song that says, "I have decided to follow Jesus," that's all **blasphemy**, all rubbish. Any decision towards Salvation is again all God's before He created this world, and no one can decide to follow Jesus, but His Children can agree to obey Him more and more each day. No one can invite Jesus into a heart. **He gives new hearts** to His Children without asking for their approval, permission, consent, or knowledge, and in His time, not yours, if at all.

Let's go to Matthew 4:18-20 NKJV *And Jesus, walking by the Sea of Galilee, saw two brothers, Simon called Peter, and Andrew his brother, casting a net into the sea; for they were fishermen. Then He said to them, "Follow Me, and I will make you fishers of men." They immediately left their nets and followed Him.* I want you to see just how Jesus chooses His Elect. Remember, the Father, Holy Spirit, and Himself appointed the Apostles before this world was created. In this verse, do you notice how Jesus, when walking, sees Peter and Andrew, who were previous followers of John the Baptist. Jesus said, **"Follow Me,"** and they dropped their nets and left them there; imagine, for a minute, that you had a fishing business, and someone comes along and says, "Follow Me," and you give up your business, drop your equipment, and just go. Let's go to Matthew 4:21-22 NKJV *Going on from there, He saw two other brothers, James the son of Zebedee, and John his brother, in the boat with Zebedee their father, mending their nets. He called them, and immediately they left the boat and their father, and followed Him.* Can you notice that Jesus called them, they followed Him, **no questions, no maybe later, no let me think about it, no nothing, no choice either, they left even their dad**, their occupation, which was their father's fishing business. They went and followed Jesus. Let's go to Matthew 9:9 NKJV *As Jesus passed on from there, He saw a man named Matthew sitting at the tax office. And He said to him, "Follow Me." So Matthew arose and followed Him.* Matthew was a tax collector, a hated man, yet a very prosperous one; he was well off, yet he left as soon as Jesus said, **"Follow Me."** We don't know whether there was any money on the table, but we know **he didn't give two weeks' notice**. No, Matthew just immediately left when Jesus said, "Follow Me." **Do you see a pattern yet?**

You cannot teach Salvation, **you cannot teach being "Born Again"** you can only give and show scripture, use The

Gospel (The Good News that God sent His Son Jesus, who was born a Virgin Birth, lived a Sinless Life was Crucified and Rose on The Third Day and LIVES) and explain it, plant a Seed, give others The Gospel and **pray God does the work,** because His Word is truly alive. It's Hebrews 4:12 NIV For *the word of God is alive and active. Sharper than any double-edged sword, it penetrates even to dividing soul and spirit, joints and marrow; it judges the thoughts and attitudes of the heart.* Here, the writer of Hebrews reveals to us a true mystery of God's Word: that **His Word alone does the Saving,** the Teaching, the instructing, the eye-opening. It is the Only Book we need; it's the Window into God. **It penetrates our Soul, our Spirit, and Judges Our Own Hearts**. What I like to do, as a friend taught me, is to give out a small Gospel of John; placing this book into someone's hand who seems receptive to what I am telling them is vital. This way, the person I attempt to witness to or share the Gospel with has God's Word in their hands; I write my phone number in it if they have any questions, and if it's a woman, my wife gives her number, so they cannot feel it's inappropriate. Now it's between them and God. **Let the Lion out!**

I will tell you of one incident that happened to me at another gym in Coral Springs, Florida. Sometimes I go to the gym, say nothing, and give no one the Gospel of John, but that day I felt the need to talk to the guy behind the counter who checked me in. I told him about Jesus, and I could see he was somewhat interested; after my workout, I went and got a small Gospel of John from my car. I went back in and gave it to him. I explained who John was and that John meticulously explains who Jesus was. Please read it, but I forgot to include my phone number. I thought nothing of it, and a week went by. I was entering that gym again around the same time this day, and this fellow was at the desk. His eyes lit up; he took me to the side and, with tears in his eyes, told me what happened. He said he was up the night before till 3 AM, and he read the Gospel of John I gave him. He said, *"God had opened my eyes to Jesus, and I am a changed man!"*

He thanked me again and again as his tears rolled down his face; I prayed with him, thanked Jesus, told this man it was ALL Him, praise God! **These are the things that go on behind the scenes. The things we know nothing about on this side of Heaven,** but we will know all in Heaven. Help those you can, spread God's Truths, even if it seems to offend, and it will. But we, as Christians, are responsible for telling others about Him and His Truths. Oh, what a joy! Let's jump over to 1 John 5:13 AMP *These things I have written to you who believe in the name of the Son of God [which represents all that Jesus Christ is and does], so that you will know [with settled and absolute knowledge] that you [already] have eternal life.* Here, John is making Salvation clear and settled in your heart, soul, and mind; stating that you should **know** you have eternal life, not that you should guess, or hope, think, but <u>KNOW</u>! This is accomplished by studying and meditating on God's Word each day, praying to Him, and letting His Word speak to your heart; it changes your heart and makes you more and more Christ-like each day. If His Word does not do that to you, **cry out to Jesus more and more each day until He hears you.**

    The Bible will tell you if you are saved or lost, if you treat others right or not, if you are doing God's Will or your own will; it tells us of our Spiritual Condition, if we are Standing In And With God or without God. The Bible Opens a Window into the Knowledge of the World, its Creation, and its End; our Birth and our Re-Birth; Heaven and Hell; how to treat our kids, our spouse, and all others throughout our lives. Yes, the **Bible does all this and more, much more. It is a Living Book, and it's a Lion, just let it out!** So, you ask, what happens to those who love God's Truths but are Not Saved? They seek Truth with all their heart, soul, and mind using the Bible, letting the Lion roar! Yes, my best life awaits me, and every Christian who loves the Lord, yet this life here will give me **persecution.** It's 2 Timothy 3:12 KJV: ***Yes, and all who desire to live godly in Christ Jesus will suffer persecution.*** Here is the answer to this chapter: *"Does God promise a better life if you choose to follow him?"*

We cannot choose to follow Him; He chooses us so that we CAN follow Him. You will lose everything but gain HIM! Amen

And Paul says it best here in Romans 8:18 KJV *For I reckon that the sufferings of this present time are not worthy to be compared with the glory which shall be revealed in us.* Paul says it all here: this present time of pain, anguish, and suffering cannot hold a candle to what God has in store for His Children in Heaven!

In Philippians 3:8 NIV, Paul says *What is more, I consider everything a loss because of the surpassing worth of knowing Christ Jesus my Lord, for whose sake I have lost all things. I consider them garbage that I may gain Christ.* **Paul is reminding us that nothing here is of any eternal value; whatever we see now is temporary and is worthless compared to Heaven, which is permanent and priceless, and awaits us. Just being in the company of Jesus, with whom we will spend eternity, oh what an unimaginable and incomprehensible joy that will be!**

Chapter 7: Is Tithing for Today's Christian?

This question has confused so many "church" goers and so-called "pastors" since the New Testament was completed. The confusion is mainly because few want to know what God's Word says about this today, but rather go along with what they heard from their previous "pastor," or "family," or "seminary" or some radio station, or TV "pastor," or a book they read, which misuses God's Word to mislead and confuse many. On the subject of tithing, many have their own preset notion of what's right. Many have already pre-determined what THEY believe and made up their mind on this whole matter, but **what does GOD say?** We must not close our eyes to **what is correct by God**, because of a closed heart, a closed mind, and a closed Bible.

I have heard all the excuses for why some buy into this lie; some say tithing, or, oh, *"I just use it as a rule of thumb."* Others say, *"Oh, there were over 20% tithes collected in the Old Testament."* Or, *"my church teaches it; what can I do about it?"* This is not even a gray area; it's as simple as **black and white**, right or wrong; it's false teaching 101 that's what it boils down to. **I have known many "Pastors" personally who have never truly studied tithing**, never challenged it, so they bought into it; *pardon the pun.* Although scripture leaves no doubt about the truth of this matter, so many "pastors" are in complete defiance and denial, truly blinded to the point of embarrassment; others **do it for the money.** Each time scripture, either in the Old or New Testament, brings up "tithing," each and every time, it is NOT concerning nor does it ever apply to today's Blood Bought Christian. **In fact, we have direct, precise, and clear scripture on just the opposite of "tithing" from The New Testament, which every Christian should want to be obedient to**...let's dig!

Some Pastors who were at odds with the Bible on this matter found clear truth from a Facebook Pastor I know, who explains tithing (every time the word is used, Old and New Testaments), all in complete detail on YouTube. So, if I don't cover it enough to declare to you the Truth of tithing in this book, since it's a mere chapter, just email me in "reference to tithing," and I will supply the link to it. But I am certain once you read this chapter, you will have no doubts as to what God's Word has to say. You should give whatever you are led to by the Holy Spirit, not man. I am saying the word "tithe"; the very word is wrong; it's using the wrong terminology, therefore **falsely instructing others** and misinterpreting scripture. Falsely using that word means that particular "church" has a false position on giving, which means they are **teaching falsely.** Words have meanings and consequences. Many Pastors just go along with tithing for **financial gain**, so let's dig in deep and see where Truth really lies. I may step on a lot of "religious" toes here, and I do not mean to offend anyone, **but truth does offend.** We are not under Mosaic Law today, but Grace. believers own nothing in this world; all we own belongs to God, not to us. We must distinguish the truth here; **there is NO tithing today!** Using the word "tithe" is erroneous. It's devious, dishonest, and deceiving. Let's dig in...

A "Tithe" is a tenth of all you make before taxes, according to some people. Yet the Biblical answer is quite simple, this is without a doubt the most abused concept damaging the "church" today. Let's start off where all false teachers want to drag you, it's Malachi 3:8-10 NIV *Will a mere mortal rob God? Yet you rob me. But you ask, How are we robbing you? In tithes and offerings.* Okay, so who is God speaking to here? He is **speaking to the Israelites, NOT the Church, NOT Blood Bought Believers!** We are under a New Covenant. The New Covenant, what we are speaking of, is found in Luke 22:20 KJV *Likewise also the cup after supper, saying, This cup is the new testament in my blood, which is shed for you.* Jesus is saying here that He is bringing in a New Covenant (New Testament) established by His Death and Resurrection, under which the Church now resides; **we are the Church, His People.** The Old Covenant is the Law of Moses, established exclusively with Israel at Mt. Sinai; it **does NOT apply to Believers**. Jewish converts to Christ are also free from the ordinances of the Law as well. Incidentally, Gentiles were never a part of the covenant made at Mt. Sinai. It was exclusively Israel's covenant.

Okay, let's continue in Galatians 5:4 GNT: *"Those of you who try to be put right with God by obeying the Law have cut yourselves off from Christ. You are outside God's grace."* Here, Paul is explaining that if someone is trying to be a "good" person, trying to live under the Law (The Old Covenant, which has been fulfilled by Christ), you have NO relationship with Jesus whatsoever. Which translates to NO relationship with God; trying to obey The Law in any capacity (to gain salvation) says you are **not His Child.** Read that verse twice! Let's jump now to Galatians 3:24 GNT *And so the Law was in charge of us until Christ came, in order that we might then be put right with God through faith.* As we see here again, that we are **no longer under the Old Covenant (The Law),** Christians are bought with the Blood of Jesus Christ, and He Satisfied and Fulfilled The Law which we could not. Jesus is our propitiation for our sins (our substitute, our atoning sacrifice). There was no other, nor will there ever be; it's Jesus or nothing.

Incidentally, the "tithe" **was always in food**, crops, or animals, **not in money**; the storehouse or Temple that housed the goods was destroyed in 70 AD. That's when tithing effectively ended. It ended then, and false teachers twist and use Eisegesis, while relying on unsupported texts and misinterpretations of scripture to confuse the unlearned, TODAY! Many are after congregational money, not merely for support; yet some are not. But those Pastors who speak the Truth about tithing (not being of today) seem to be debt-free; it looks like honesty does pay. Also, if a Child of God teaches or condones such error knowingly, woe to that man; he will be held accountable by God. Those so-called "pastors" who are seemingly rich because of being a "pastor," note the small "p," are workers for their daddy, Satan! Yet there are a few Pastors who just don't know this simple Truth. Hence, this book, I pray it may lead you to areas of Truth you didn't know existed, but God knew. Keep reading. God is good.

The food (tithes) collected went to the Old Testament Priest, so they wouldn't have to return to farming. The purpose of the storehouse was for the sustenance of the **Priests and the Levites, not for any upkeep or funding of "church" ministries.** Okay, so now you understand what the New Covenant Believers are under. Let's jump over to Acts 18:2-4 GNT. *Paul went to see them, and stayed and worked with them, because he **earned his living by making tents**, just as they did. He held discussions in the synagogue every Sabbath, trying to convince both Jews and Greeks.* Here we read that Paul (the Apostle who wrote ¾ of the New Testament) and the Apostle Luke, the writer of the Book of Acts, explain **Paul's profession: tent-making (leather trade). He made tents for a living to earn money.** Paul, the Apostle of Jesus, **didn't pass around a hat, bucket, or plate to collect money** each Saturday when he preached. Let me reiterate here that when Jesus Himself Preached to the five thousand and then the four thousand, He didn't pass a hat, bucket, or plate around either, but He did feed them all by passing baskets around! Jesus fed them all and collected nothing; neither did His Apostles teach tithing, nor did they collect any money as an exchange for those baskets of food. **So, why is tithing even spoken of today? Either it's greed, ignorance, or both!** If your "pastor" says to tithe, show him in God's Word where he is mistaken, or give him a copy of this book, or politely explain to him yourself, always start by using 2 Timothy 3:16 so there is a foundation of correction. Here's the verse one last time 2 Timothy 3:16 GNT *All Scripture is inspired by God and is useful for teaching the truth, rebuking error, correcting faults, and giving instruction for right living* Ask him to show you using scripture where tithing is taught in The New Testament concerning todays Blood Bought Believers and he will only try and trick you by confusing you with unrelated verses, such is expected from a polished charlatan.

Jesus could have collected large amounts of money by passing a bucket and collecting from the crowds, yet He never did. Remember this: God wants your Heart, all of it. It is okay to see to it that your "pastor" can earn a living inside the "church" without working a job; serving the Lord is the highest calling; thus, **offerings** are reasonable and in order, and is the proper terminology. There are bills to be paid, which is understandable. **But when a "pastor" asks you or instructs you to tithe, correct him or find a Bible-believing church.** Let's get back to where these false teachers always go and camp out there a minute, it's Malachi 3:9 KJV *Ye are cursed with a curse: for ye have robbed me, even this whole nation.* **Here we see God NOT speaking to New Covenant Blood Bought Believers but to the Nation of Israel;** today's so-called "pastors" always leave that part of the verse out. Jump with me over to Galatians 3:13 KJV *Christ hath redeemed us from the curse of the law, being made a curse for us: for it is written, Cursed is every one that hangeth on a tree:* Here we see that Christ Paid and Absorbed That Curse. Christians are bought with the Highest Price Ever; the Perfect Life of Jesus the Christ. **There are NO curses that could ever apply to Believers** after that. Let's go over to the verse that clears this whole misconception up and answers definitively and conclusively the question pertaining to this chapter, "Is tithing for today's Christian?" It's **2 Corinthians KJV 9:7 *Every man according as he purposeth in his heart, so let him give; not grudgingly, or of necessity: for God loveth a cheerful giver.*** Let's unpack this most revealing Truth concerning giving. Here, Paul is teaching the Corinthian Church, which was composed of both Gentiles and Jewish people. What did Paul teach? **Tithing? NO, Paul taught the exact opposite of tithing.** He taught them and is teaching us today that Believers are to give as they feel in their hearts, not reluctantly or out of obligation, for God loves a cheerful giver (the Greek word used here is Hilaros, which means "hilarious"; be hilarious in your giving). God loves a Hilarious Giver! Remember, giving is to God, not man, and for the Believer, that means using God's wisdom. If one's heart is right with God, the Holy Spirit will prompt one accordingly in one's giving because of one's new heart, which belongs to

God. **Now there is giving of time, talent, or service, as well as monetary support.** If you are not on board with what your "church" is collecting money for, **give nothing! You may also examine the "churches" books to see where all monies are being spent.** There should be a monthly bulletin or newsletter at most honest "churches" explaining where all collected monies end up and what they're used for. If you are getting fed Truth, support your Church. How else can they keep their doors open? Being a good steward is important. The verse to give to your "pastor" if he says "we are now collecting your tithes and offerings" is 2 Corinthians KJV 9:7 *Every man according as he purposeth in his heart, so let him give; not grudgingly, or of necessity: for God loveth a cheerful giver.* Then ask him, **"What part of this verse don't you understand?"** If he disagrees with you or twists that verse to mean tithing is of today, don't be bamboozled; **leave that "church!"** It would be easier for a camel to go through the eye of a needle than to teach that man God's Truths. It should not matter if he is your friend; every Believer should correct a "Brother" who is wrong. We should always correct each other, it's Proverbs 27:17 ESV *Iron sharpens iron and one man sharpens another.* No man is above you, so as not correct him. Let's visit Proverbs 9:8 NIV *Do not rebuke mockers, or they will hate you; rebuke the wise, and they will love you.* **Here we see that using God's wisdom, a wise man will love you when you correct him, just hope your "pastor" is a wise man; if not, you may be looking for a new church, and rightfully so.** Also, remember it's the duty of every Believer to expose false teaching and **false teachers**; false teaching causes confusion. Confusion is never from God, but from Satan. Reveal your "pastors" wrongs to him personally, and he will correct his wrongs and honor God in doing so; such are true men of God.

In 2 Corinthians 9:7, God is actually saying He loves, a Cheerful Giver, give from your heart what makes YOU happy (as led by The Holy Spirit, which lives in ALL Believers) and give what you are **able** and willing to give. **The more you** give is **NOT** the more you get; never buy into any "prosperity gospel." I feel that the Bible is clear that we should help widows, orphans, the homeless, and our neighbors (think of the story of the Good Samaritan). Helping others is Christ-like. Jesus came as a servant for many. **He healed thousands and thousands, yet had only 120 (one hundred and twenty) true Believers when He was crucified.** And again, if you are in a "church" that is asking or demanding your tithe, I suggest you teach or inform that "pastor" of the Biblical Truth of Giving, make him accountable to God's Word, or **leave** that false teaching "church." We, as Christians, must also realize why these "churches" push or even mention tithing: they either have a tradition of it because their daddy's "church" did it, or their "pastor" did it, or their "seminary" taught them incorrectly. They may have huge debts which they service; maybe a "church" mortgage; others have private airplanes, bodyguards, multiple homes, big light shows, big bands, smoke machines, and staff; well, think of what Jesus had. **Think of how little the Apostles had**; few will want the Truths written in this book, **greed and pride take over in an unregenerate heart.** Many "pastors" know the Truth of tithing and ask their congregation anyway, **which is EVIL** and very deceitful; and **if they don't know, they are too ill-informed, confused, or misinformed to teach others anyway!** What else are they mistaken about? Are you attending that "church" to grow in false teaching? Sadly, most parishioners know so little of God's Word, they yield to their "pastors" false teaching; thus, this book, I pray...God willing, it opens closed eyes.

Let me further elaborate: WE as Christians are always told by many to act and be Christ-like, and rightly so. **So, why would we "tithe" if Jesus never once tithed?** Okay, many say, let's do as God's Word instructs, and rightly so; it teaches new Covenant Believers to give as they feel led by the Holy Spirit, and rightfully so. Many others say, let's do as the Apostles, Chosen and taught personally by Jesus, in what's right to do; and rightfully so; **none of them tithed** and none of them taught others to tithe either. **Every false teacher out there is identified by pushing the "tithe", why?** Yes, this is where all false teachers start, and therefore, it's become very easy to identify them; they expose themselves by asking their parishioners to tithe. At the same time, they also expose themselves as false converts to the educated Christian, the one who studies God's Word, His Elect. Okay, let's do the math; if the "church" you attend has 400 parishioners attending and each tithe, let's say they all make minimum wage, for this example. Let's say $320 per week each (which is very low), that's $128,000 per week, and 10% of that is $12,800 per week to this "church," which is $51,200 a month, which is $614,000 a year! Okay, let's say your "church" has 4000 members, that amount is now $1,280,000 a week, and that's $5,120,000 per month or over ($61,440,000.) OVER 61 million dollars a year! Do you see why it's financially rewarding to keep parishioners in the dark? Again, if "churches" taught the truth on this, I feel they would not only be pleasing God by being Biblically correct and having a clean conscience, but parishioners would also give more freely, joyfully, and hilariously! **Truth matters!**

Biblical tithing is not found anywhere in the New Testament (each time it's mentioned, it's NOT applicable to the Blood Bought Believer). But that won't stop the creative mind, the one stuck on greed or tradition. Let's say your "pastor" is innocent; he is not aware of this truth. Okay, that's a stretch, but even if he is unaware, Paul writing to the Colossians spoke of tradition, it's Colossians 2:8 (KJV) *Beware lest any man spoil you through **philosophy and vain deceit, after the tradition of men,** after the rudiments of the world, and not after Christ.* Paul is teaching how this world and its false teachers will deceive many with what seems to be right, yet it's just their own smokescreen, ignorance, **tradition**, or **greed**, which are used to indoctrinate you (teach a one-sided opinion) of their own views; cults and **false religions, along with false teachers, all use such deception.** They teach false giving practices based on misinterpretations and the twisting of the true meaning of scripture, to say what they want it to, remember it's called EISEGESIS (making text say what a false teacher wants it to), but the right way to teach is using EXEGESIS (to draw out the truth using the text correctly).

Let's jump over to Matthew 6:1-4 (NKJV) *"Take heed that you do not do your charitable deeds before men, to be seen by them. Otherwise you have no reward from your Father in heaven. Therefore, when you do a charitable deed, do not sound a trumpet before you as the hypocrites do in the synagogues and in the streets, that they may have glory from men. Assuredly, I say to you, they have their reward. But when you do a charitable deed, do not let your left hand know what your right hand is doing, that your charitable deed may be in secret; and your Father who sees in secret will Himself reward you openly.* Here we see Jesus preaching the Sermon on the Mount. **Here, Jesus is teaching the act of giving. Did He Teach "tithing?"...NO, He Did NOT.** Jesus said, not to let others know what or how much you are to give to anyone (at any time) concerning helping the poor, the homeless, the widows, orphans, all giving, any giving which would also include your local "church." Jesus says NOT to sound a trumpet; meaning don't brag of your giving, don't brag if you give all you have away. Jesus goes on to say this is what hypocrites do, and those who brag or push to get your "tithe" or even mention that word; they are wrong to do so as well, they go directly against what Jesus is teaching! Jesus says, *"Give in secret, and you will be rewarded by God openly."* How is any "pastor" who mentions, demands, or even asks for 10% of your salary being honest?

Many professions and their salaries are public knowledge; asking for your 10% is not a secret, but openly known; so, asking for 10% of your salary is giving in secret? Some "churches" at the end of each "tax year" give or send you a contribution or donation receipt. How is that giving in secret? **Do you see how unbiblical tithing is?** This goes directly against what Jesus preached! By giving to "churches" in this way, **God is not out to bless you; you are doing as a man in error told you, as tradition**

instructs. God does not bless stupidity. Why do you think giving a certain amount, because someone told you to, someone other than God through His Word, will bless you? To rightly divide His Word, let's look again at 2 Timothy 2:15 (KJV) *Study to shew thyself approved unto God, a workman that needeth not to be ashamed, rightly dividing the word of truth.* To be approved and accepted by God is to study and discern GOD'S WORD accurately, correctly, NOT incorrectly, any fool can and will do that! If you are a true Child of God, you will settle for nothing less than GOD'S TRUTH.

Correct obedience brings blessings, not by listening and obeying false teachers or condoning their verbal mistakes, misdirection, and mindsets that are in error. Why go or teach against scripture? If you are a Child of God, He will open your eyes through His Word, this book, and others like it, to bring His Truths to the surface to bless you, correct you, rebuke, and reprimand you. **Remember, going against Scripture would be to tithe; to buy into or tolerate such terminology, or jargon would mean you are listening to false teaching and accepting it** means you will possibly be adhering to it, or buy into it; then one day you too may even teach it! God forbid...That's how misnomers, lies, and the false teachings of God's Word spread. It is never wise to go against God's Word to make others happy; buying into any Biblical falsehood once the truth is exposed and brought to your attention is very, very unwise!

Whatever you give, wherever and however you give, take no receipt; for that receipt is your reward; **giving to God is NOT a tax write off! That "write off" because of your ignorance of God's Word is your reward from God.** Giving to organizations "so you can say, you tithe, or give" such as in today's "churches," is NOT what God meant by giving. Look at all giving as charity; do you ask a homeless man for a receipt? **Your lack of discernment is dishonoring God.** Do you think God rewards ignorance in giving? **Do YOU believe truth in all areas matters to God?** Do you think studying His Word, seeking His truth, is important to Him? If not, keep listening to the false teachers who will tickle your ears. I will not...I will continue to study God's Word to rightly divide it, and so should YOU...Is it time to do some imaginary rhetorical proverbial finger-pointing? Have you bought into the tithing lie? Don't! Turn to Matthew 6:1-4 LSB *"Beware of doing your righteousness before men to be noticed by them; otherwise you have no reward with your Father who is in heaven. Therefore, when you give to the poor, do not sound a trumpet before you, **as the hypocrites do** in the synagogues and in the streets, so that they may be glorified by men. Truly, I say to you, they have their reward in full. But when you give to the poor, do not let your left hand know what your right hand is doing, so that your **giving will be in secret**; and your Father who sees what is done in secret will reward you.* **Jesus teaches how to give, keeping it a secret from everyone! Those who don't, their accolades from men are their reward. God will NOT be mocked. Don't be like the hypocrites who seek praise from men for their giving!**

Christians are living under Grace, Grace, and Grace; let's look at John 8:36 KJV, yet another Election verse. *If the Son therefore shall make you free, ye shall be free indeed.* Jesus says if **HE** makes you free, YOU are free; therefore, **His Children are NOT subject to any curses, NOT subject to The Law, NOT subject to tithing,** but He Commanded us to do many other things, which brings us to our next Chapter! Let's keep digging...

Chapter 8: Should we Judge others?

This is something the world usually throws at Christians, yet many Believers were not taught the Bible correctly. Let's dig in... Were you ever scolded by someone saying, "Who are you to judge?" or "Only God can judge me?" Or did someone ever throw scripture at you, "Judge not, that ye not be judged?" The word "judge" is in the Bible as (Judges, judgment(s), judging, judgeth) over 700 times. With one whole book entitled Judges, it was written at a time when God raised up Judges to lead His People.

Let's begin in Matthew 7:1-6 ESV: *"Judge not, that you be not judged. For with the judgment you pronounce you will be judged, and with the measure you use it will be measured to you. Why do you see the speck that is in your brother's eye, but do not notice the log that is in your own eye? Or how can you say to your brother, 'Let me take the speck out of your eye,' when there is the log in your own eye? You hypocrite, first take the log out of your own eye, and then you will see clearly to take the speck out of your brother's eye. Do not give dogs what is holy, and do not throw your pearls before pigs, lest they trample them underfoot and turn to attack you."* Let's unpack these six verses. Here, Jesus is preaching the most popular sermon of all time, The Sermon on the Mount.

He is explaining and teaching the right way to judge. He says, "In the way you judge, you too will be judged." What is He saying? **This is why no one should take a verse out of context and throw it around as if they know what the true meaning is.** Jesus elaborates, if you have that same sin, for instance, let's say you are an alcoholic and your friend stops to see you and has a beer in his hand, and you tell him he needs to stop drinking, yet that was his first beer in a year, and you consume a 6-pack a day! This works with every sin, if you yourself are guilty of something (a sin) and you call out someone else about their wrong (their sin, that sin), first repent and correct yourself of that sin, your wrong. First, clean up your sin, don't be a hypocrite; get right with God in that area, and then help your friend with his sin. If he is a liar and you tell him that, but are you a liar yourself? Remove that particular sin from your life before you can help another with theirs. **He goes on to explain, judging by judging, he is a Brilliant Teacher, teaching us to do it righteously.** He says, "Don't give to dogs what is Holy." What does He mean? He is teaching us to use discernment towards what is Holy. Here, Jesus is speaking of God's Word; to **know whether one is a DOG or a PIG, one must FIRST JUDGE THEM.** If you give someone whom you discern to be a dog or pig any correction or the Gospel, when you know he or she may turn on you or kill you, just don't do it. **There is no reward from God for stupidity.**

Let's look at Amos 5:14-15 NKJV *Seek good and not evil, that you may live; so the Lord God of hosts will be with you, as you have spoken. **Hate evil, love good;** Establish justice in the gate...* How can we hate the evil and love the good if we refuse to judge? **Actually, we go against God when we refuse to judge others righteously.** We live in a civilization where everyone today says, oh, just love, love, love. It's a very tolerant society; many condone other people's choices and lifestyles as correct, even if they are self-destructive, life-threatening, or lacking any moral fiber. It seems arrogant, close-minded, racist, or bigoted to even correct someone today, in this increasingly hostile world, when the opposite is true. If I saw your kid running after a ball that rolled into the street and I went and yelled at him, even grabbed him or her violently, because a passing bus would have surely killed that child; therefore, I saved his or her life, would that kid's parents be happy or mad at me? This is the same scenario as far as God is concerned. To NOT tell someone who obviously is headed for a crash, headed in the wrong direction with their thinking or actions on a path to Hell; NOT giving them your warning, about God's Truth, about what GOD calls a sin, is in itself a SIN. **Your silence is a sin, and yes, not judging them is a sin**. If you had a chance to save my little girl and you said nothing and did nothing and that bus rolled over her, **I would come after**

you! Look at it this way, **to warn someone of eternal consequences is NOT judging them; it's loving them!** <u>With God, we are all responsible for what we do and say, and for what we don't do and don't say as well</u>. It would be wiser to stand up at ALL times for God's Truths, than to ever side with the world in any area where God's Word is in clear opposition. **You will lose family, friends, and look like a separatist because if you are a Child of God, that's exactly what you are, separate from this world. Why fight this truth?** Be the Light... God is watching; it's best to please Him over anyone else. Truth in all areas of God's Word is important, very important! Martin Luther, a German Monk who began the Protestant Reformation in the 16th century, said, *"Always preach in such a way that if the people listening do not come to hate their sin, they will instead hate you."* So true, Brother Martin!

Let's visit John 7:24 KJV: *Judge not according to the appearance, but judge righteous judgment.* Here, Jesus is teaching again to judge, but not if one is a better dresser than another or one is poorer than another, but **judge rightly according to Biblical Judgment using God's Standards**, not yours. Let's give a look at 1 Corinthians 1:10 KJV *Now I beseech you, brethren, by the name of our Lord Jesus Christ, that ye all speak the same thing, and that there be no divisions among you; but that ye be perfectly joined together in the same mind and in the same judgment.* Here, Paul is addressing the Church in Corinth; to be all on the same page, in unison, without divisions, joined together in one mind, and we all should JUDGE the same because we all should use the Word of God to do so. **True unity is only built upon sound Doctrine and correct Theology.** Let's open up 1 Corinthians 2:14-16 NKJV *But the natural man does not receive the things of the Spirit of God, for they are foolishness to him; nor can he know them, because they are spiritually discerned. But he who is spiritual judges all things, yet he himself is rightly judged by no one. For "who has known the mind of the Lord that he may instruct Him?" But we have the mind of Christ.* Here, Paul teaches, through his first letter to

111

the Corinthians, why some understand, and others do not. The natural man is the unsaved man; the unbelieving man (non-elect) who cannot receive the teachings and insights of the Lord because being dead spiritually means God has not opened that person's eyes. But the one who God has opened their eyes, The Saved, The Born Again, God's Children, and therefore by using God's Standards **is allowed and commanded to judge all things,** and no one who is not of God could challenge such wisdom, for it is of God; be a spiritually mature Christian. This is what God wants for all His Children. **When true Christians tell someone a hard Truth, he or she is trying to free that person from a prison they don't even know they're in. Remember, the Truth does not change according to our ability to stomach it.**

Believers are able to know and have the Mind of Christ by studying and being saturated in God's Truths each day. Believers don't go with the flow; they stand firm in God's Word. This confronts a culture that hates objective Truth, especially when it stands in direct opposition to the essence of our age and the secular way in which people reason and live in this twisted world. What comes to mind here, before I close this chapter, is to reiterate that **false teachers, advancing the misuse of God's Word, should be exposed by name** to all who would listen to know the Truth. One must know scripture to expose these charlatans and counterfeits, those who are out and about using God's Word like Satan did, by taking a verse or two out of context, and twisting the true meaning, like those who call for tithes, just to confuse the unlearned towards their own financial gain. Yet if these so-called "pastors" were to tell the Truth about giving and NOT use the word tithing, their congregation may give much more. God sometimes rewards the liars (false teachers) because most of the time, they're not God's Children, but Satan's, so God may allow it. **Why, you ask? Because that "pastor" is a punishment to those who listen to him for not studying His Word; remember Jesus said to many, "Haven't You Read?"**

1 Corinthians 6:1-3 KJV *Dare any of you, having a matter against another, go to law before the unjust, and not before the saints? Do ye not know that the saints shall judge the world? and if the world shall be judged by you, are ye unworthy to judge the smallest matters? Know ye not that we shall judge angels? how much more things that pertain to this life?* Here, Paul rebukes them in his teachings, explaining that any matter against another before the law refers to a civil dispute with another Believer. Paul says, *"Why would you go to court before unrighteous men, non-believers?"* Christians should place their issues before other Saints and other Believers and work out their differences that way. Paul goes on to explain that Believers will one day judge the World; he therefore urges you to be competent and capable of judging petty cases or trivial worldly matters. The Apostle Paul continues to open the window to our future, saying **we will also one day judge the Angels.** Oh, what an insight into our Glorious Everlasting Future! Let's jump to Ephesians 5:11 KJV *And have no fellowship with the unfruitful works of darkness, but rather reprove them.* What Paul is teaching here is that we should have nothing to do with evil, nothing to do with the ways of the world which are against the Word of God. We must expose them, not just sit. I have heard many "so-called believers" say, "Oh, God has that; He will take care of this or that." What these people don't understand is that they must be responsible and accountable as Christians, representing all truths. That's why God placed YOU where He placed you. To do His Work, His Bidding, bring His Word of Righteousness to others, His Gospel, His Ways, and Rebuke the ways man has adopted as right when they are the opposite of what's right. Why do so many "so-called believers" just sit, because they are "make-believers", not true Believers, **true Believers speak up, stand out, and are typically hated, because darkness wants nothing to do with Light.**

It's now John 3:19 NKJV *And this is the condemnation, that the light has come into the world, and men loved darkness rather than light, because their deeds were evil.*

Here we see the crisis this world is in. God sent Jesus, He is The Light, The Life, The Truth, and The Way, but men and women everywhere would rather run to the darkness, or their self-proclaimed righteousness. Those who run to darkness or that which is wrong in God's Eyes aren't at all interested in pleasing God. They are in denial, living in a state of delusion, thinking they are right and God's Ways are foolish and obsolete. But those who love the Lord work within God's Truths, His Ways, and are disgusted by the world's view. Let's confirm what I said earlier: God is the same yesterday, today, and tomorrow. It's Hebrews 13:8 KJV: *Jesus Christ the same yesterday, and today, and forever.* This way, there is no confusion about Jesus thinking one way in eternity past, another way today, and another when He walked the earth. JESUS was okay with taking out the whole world with a flood because of its wickedness, He was okay with the destruction of Sodom and Gomorrah because of their homosexuality, and yes, He Himself will come again to judge the Entire World, dividing the Righteous from the Wicked.

Let's dig into 2 Peter 2:20-22 KJV *For if after they have escaped the pollutions of the world through the knowledge of the Lord and Savior Jesus Christ, they are again entangled therein, and overcome, the latter end is worse with them than the beginning. For it had been better for them not to have known the way of righteousness, than, after they have known it, to turn from the holy commandment delivered unto them. But it is happened unto them according to the true proverb, The dog is turned to his own vomit again; and the sow that was washed to her wallowing in the mire.* Here, Peter explains a common condition that we see all too often from "false pastors" and "fake Christians" alike. If, after escaping from the slum of sin by experiencing the Truths of the Lord and Savior Jesus, one slides back into their same old life again. Peter says they are in worse condition than if they had never left the slums. Then Peter quotes a well-known Proverb 26:11 KJV *As a dog returneth to his vomit, so a fool returneth to his folly.* Meaning such a person goes back to what they were once removed from, their slum, their corruption, their evil, their liberal ideology, and returns to it, worldly again. The foolishness of turning back to their vomit, their past, their old life; **such a person was never born again by God, but self-deceived.**

The above verse will come to a brighter light if I close this Chapter by first going through the Parable of the Sower, Luke 8:4-15 NIV. *While a large crowd was gathering and people were coming to Jesus from town after town, he told this parable: "A farmer went out to sow his seed. As he was scattering the seed, some fell along the path; it was trampled on, and the birds ate it up. Some fell on rocky ground, and when it came up, the plants withered because they had no moisture. Other seed fell among thorns, which grew up with it and choked the plants. Still other seed fell on good soil. It came up and yielded a crop, a hundred times more than was sown." When he said this, he called out, "Whoever has ears to hear, let them hear." His disciples asked him what this parable meant. He said, "The knowledge of the secrets of the kingdom of God has been given to you, but to others I speak in parables, so that though seeing, they may not see; though hearing, they may not understand". "This is the meaning of the parable: The seed is the word of God. Those along the path are the ones who hear, and then the devil comes and takes away the word from their hearts, so that they may NOT believe and be saved. Those on the rocky ground are the ones who receive the word with joy when they hear it, but they have no root. They believe for a while, but in the time of testing they fall away. The seed that fell among thorns stands for those who hear, but as they go on their way they are choked by life's worries, riches and pleasures, and they do not mature. But the seed on good soil stands for those with a noble and good heart, who hear the word, retain it, and by persevering produce a crop".* **Wow, Jesus unravels the mysteries of His Truths** concerning why so many seem to believe. And why are many not so sure, while others turn 180% and return to their vomit?

Let's look at these twelve verses, which are packed with God's insights. Before Jesus went on to explain His Parable, what is a "parable"? A Parable is an analogy (not a true story), which is a comparison between two things to obscure a story or clarify one. Why would Jesus use parables, which He does from that verse on, so His Disciples would understand and Believers alike (once they were given The Holy Spirit), but also so unbelievers would not see. Jesus said, *"The knowledge of the secrets of the kingdom of God has been given to you, but to others I speak in parables."* He is doing this because of His Mercy and His Judgment. Jesus uses parables to obscure the Truth from unbelievers while making it clear to His Disciples; it's a judgment because He keeps unbelievers in the darkness they enjoy so much, and it's a mercy because any further exposure to Truth would only increase their condemnation. Now look at this same verse again, John 3:19 NKJV *And this is the condemnation, that the light has come into the world, and men loved darkness rather than light, because their deeds were evil.* This is a hard pill to swallow, but then again, **God's Word is Light, and if you love His Truths, His Light, then you are His Child, rejoice!** There is no need for me to attempt to interpret or further explain what Jesus Himself has already done in those 12 verses; **The Master Himself explains them**. I will simply add this: The Seed (Word of God) in the last verse says, "The Ones Who Hear." Yes, The Ones Who Hear, and Do as He Commands are His; those are The Elect.

Chapter 9: Did Jonah Preach with Hate?

This chapter will be an eye-opener. We as Christians tend to believe that only kind and loving words would lead someone to Christ and His Salvation. And I don't doubt that is the best approach to God's Gospel. But today's "pastors" go too far; they form groups, clubs, and use entertainment in place of GOD'S Own Words Straight Out of The Bible. Remember **God's Word is a Living Word;** it's not dead like other books written by men because the Bible is God-breathed. So today we have "pastors" tickling the ears of parishioners (church goers) and telling them just what won't hurt their feelings, **just enough to not offend anyone, keeping peace with all unbelievers**, that's why unbelievers are confused about their "salvation." They won't speak of repentance or self-denial. **They may be popular "pastors," but they are false teachers.** That's why I see and find mostly unbelievers going to "churches" today, some for 10 years without even knowing or understanding a foundation of Biblical Truths. It is better they know the Truth then to live a lie. **If real preaching creates real converts, it also eliminates fake Christians, and rightfully so.**

If real Pastors preach God's Truths, most would not want anything to do with the God of the Bible. That's why so many create their own "god" in their minds, one who loves all their sin and accepts it, turning a blind eye away from it in place of repentance from it. This is solely because of weak watered-down (free will salvation) gospels that are NOT the true "gospel" at all. Many, in place of the Jesus of the Bible, have a "jesus" of their own making, and they teach others the same false "jesus," and this domino effect doesn't end until a True Believer says, "What's Wrong with You Guys!" **And points a finger and says NO!** And sends them over to that verse on my wall, 2 Timothy 3:16 ESV *All Scripture is breathed out by God and profitable for teaching, for reproof, for correction, and for training in righteousness.* This is worth repeating twice in this book, and using it will clear up the confusion in "churches" worldwide. 1 Corinthians 14:33 KJV

For God is not the author of confusion, but of peace, as in all churches of the saints. Here, Paul tells us where peace comes from: it comes from God and His People, for we are The Church and His Saints forevermore. Then the opposite is true, where does evil, confusion, misunderstandings, misinterpretations, delusions, misbeliefs, and wrong teachings come from? **They all come from within the unconverted heart and from Satan and his demons.** Now Satan, aka "Father of Lies" or "Evil One" or "Enemy" or "Devil" or "Deceiver" or "Antichrist" or "Angel of Light" or "Accuser," here are just a few of the names Satan goes by. Don't think that Satan has to involve himself in an unbeliever's life just to cause havoc. The unregenerate heart (one of the world, an unbeliever), because of human depravity, needs no help to be evil; it's their nature. Just remember who their daddy is, Satan. You see, before I was saved, I had many more years with my liberal progressive perverted daddy, Satan, than I had with my Righteous, Conservative Holy, Heavenly Father, so that old influence was there. But now it has been replaced by God's Word. Remember, we are still in our flesh, but the Holy Spirit within us does His Redemptive Work, Giving Us a New Conscience, yet we sin. I tell those who ask me, "Do you still sin?" I reply, *"I am not sinless, but I sin much, much less."* When I do sin, it burdens the Holy Spirit in me; I run to Jesus and confess it to my Lord, Repent and keep moving forward. Always get up and run back to Jesus, not to sin, and not to the world.

Let's jump over to John 8:44 ESV *You are of your father the devil, and your will is to do your father's desires. He was a murderer from the beginning, and does not stand in the truth, because there is no truth in him. When he lies, he speaks out of his own character, for he is a liar and the father of lies.* Jesus explains that even our condition before God, when we were saved. We all took on the nature and characteristics of Satan because he, too, was once our father, but for God and His Mercy shown to His Children, who have a New Nature in Jesus. Now let's consider Jonah 1:1-17 GNT *One day the Lord spoke to Jonah son of Amittai. He said, "Go to Nineveh, that great city, and speak out against it; I am aware of how wicked its people are." Jonah, however, set out in the opposite direction in order to get away from the Lord. He went to Joppa, where he found a ship about to go to Spain. He paid his fare and went aboard with the crew to sail to Spain, where he would be away from the Lord. But the Lord sent a strong wind on the sea, and the storm was so violent that the ship was in danger of breaking up. The sailors were terrified and cried out for help, each one to his own god. Then, in order to lessen the danger, they threw the cargo overboard. Meanwhile, Jonah had gone below and was lying in the ship's hold, sound asleep. The captain found him there and said to him, "What are you doing asleep? Get up and pray to your god for help. Maybe he will feel sorry for us and spare our lives."*

The sailors said to each other, "Let's draw lots and find out who is to blame for getting us into this danger." They did so, and Jonah's name was drawn. So they said to him, "Now, then, tell us! Who is to blame for this? What are you doing here? What country do you come from? What is your nationality?" "I am a Hebrew," Jonah answered. "I worship the Lord, the God of Heaven, who made land and sea." Jonah went on to tell them that he was running away from the Lord. The sailors were terrified, and said to him, "That was an awful thing to do!" The storm was getting worse all the time, so the sailors asked him, "What should we do to you to stop the storm?" Jonah answered, "Throw me into the sea, and it will calm down. I know it is my fault that you are caught in this violent storm." Instead, the sailors tried to get the ship to shore, rowing with all their might. But the storm was becoming worse and worse, and they got nowhere. So they cried out to the Lord, "O Lord, we pray, don't punish us with death for taking this man's life! You, O Lord, are responsible for all this; it is your doing." Then they picked Jonah up and threw him into the sea, and it calmed down at once. This made the sailors so afraid of the Lord that they offered a sacrifice and promised to serve him. At the Lord's command a large fish swallowed Jonah, and he was inside the fish for three days and three nights.

Here in Jonah chapter one, we see the rebellious Jonah going in the opposite direction God told him to go, because he hated the wicked Ninevites. Jonah wanted nothing to do with what God wanted; he tried to avoid God, but **running from God is never wise.** He almost got others killed on the ship because of His disobedience. **Trying to flee from God's Will, as we shall see, is absolutely impossible.** They drew lots on the ship (like drawing straws, possibly using stones) to see whose fault the supernatural storm was; of course, God made it known that Jonah would be at fault. They threw Jonah off the ship, as Jonah suggested, and the sea became calm as soon as Jonah left it. Then those on the ship feared Jonah's God. **God was always in control**; yet He was chastising Jonah, remember that's what God does when His Children are disobedient. So, Jonah spent three days in a large fish, as written also in Matthew 12:40 ESV *For just as Jonah was three days and three nights in the belly of the great fish, so will the Son of Man be three days and three nights in the heart of the earth.* Jesus is telling them of Jonah and the three days Jonah spent in the big fish's belly. Jesus is telling the Pharisees what will happen to Him, yet they did not get it. Back to Jonah 2:1-2 GNT *from deep inside the fish Jonah prayed to the Lord his God: "In my distress, **O Lord, I called to you, and you answered me**. From deep in the <u>world of the dead</u> I cried for help, and you heard me."* Jonah cried out to God, and he was regurgitated from the whale's belly onto land. <u>Jonah cried out</u> from the <u>world of the dead</u>. I want to take time here to further explain this "world of the dead". Here the word Sheol, which is in The Old Testament details it; as to refer to the grave or the abode of the dead, unlike this world; Sheol in the Bible which is devoid of a full description, but there is no light Job 14:13 ESV *Oh that you would **hide me in Sheol**, that you would conceal me until your wrath be past, that you would appoint me a set time, and remember me!* Here Job gives us some information that it is a place, not Heaven and not Hell, <u>there is NO ONE IN HELL as of yet, because Judgment Day has not arrived yet</u>. So, where are the Lost who have died so far?

Sheol (the unseen world) is where my study brings me. Let's jump to Psalms 16:10 NKJV *For You will not leave my soul in Sheol, Nor will You allow Your Holy One to see corruption.* Here King David is asking God not to let him remain in Sheol (Hades), the abode of the dead, or the grave, but points to The Holy One, Who is to come; he points prophetically or predictively to **Jesus's Future Resurrection**. See Acts 2:25-27 NKJV *For David says concerning Him: "I foresaw the Lord always before my face, For He is at my right hand, that I may not be shaken. Therefore my heart rejoiced, and my tongue was glad; Moreover my flesh also will rest in hope. **For You will not leave my soul in Hades, Nor will You allow Your Holy One to see corruption.**"* We see King David referring to Hades, a term used many times throughout the Bible; it's a place or state where all the dead exist. In the parable of the rich man and Lazarus, the rich man experiences torment in Hades. **This is an intermediate state for the lost until Judgement Day.** Let's look at when Lazarus (Jesus's friend) died; go to John 11:39-44 NLT *"Roll the stone aside," Jesus told them. But Martha, the dead man's sister, protested, "Lord, he has been dead for four days. The smell will be terrible." Jesus responded, "Didn't I tell you that you would see God's glory if you believe?" So they rolled the stone aside. Then Jesus looked up to heaven and said, "Father, thank you for hearing me. You always hear me, but I said it out loud for the sake of all these people standing here, so that they will believe you sent me." Then Jesus shouted, "Lazarus, come out!" And the dead man came out, his hands and feet bound in grave clothes, his face wrapped in a head cloth. Jesus told them, "Unwrap him and let him go!"* Here we see the Unlimited Power of God, but where did Lazarus go for four days? Some say "soul sleep," a state of not knowing or feeling anything until you are woken, somewhat like a coma without any dreams; stillness, where time and space do not exist. Let's continue to break it down. He didn't go to Heaven; Jesus hadn't yet been resurrected from His grave, yet (Jesus wouldn't bring him back to Earth from such a glorious place).

He didn't go to Hell; no one is there yet (Hell will be occupied after Christ's Millennium (1000-year reign) on Earth). **Get my book "Examine The End Times" to better understand future events.** Not Gehenna, which is the Greek word for Hell. Not Hades, a place where evil occupants will be judged prior to entering the lake of fire (Hell), reserved for the lost, those without Christ. Let's look at Revelation 20:13-15 NJKV *The sea gave up the dead who were in it, and Death and Hades delivered up the dead who were in them. And they were judged, each one according to his works. Then Death and Hades were cast into the lake of fire. This is the second death. And anyone not found written in the Book of Life was cast into the lake of fire.* As we see here, through a process of elimination, I would say, Sheol, which could be translated as the grave; this is where again my study brings me; yet the Bible is silent on where Lazarus's (soul) went, but we know where his body was. I think he must have been asked by his whole family and friends, *"Lazarus, where were you for four days? What do you remember?"* One day, we may ask him personally. Moreover, nothing is impossible with God.

Let's go to Matthew 25:31-35 KJV When *the Son of man shall come in his glory, and all the holy angels with him, then shall he sit upon the throne of his glory: And before him shall be gathered all nations: and he shall separate them one from another, as a shepherd divideth his sheep from the goats: And he shall set the sheep on his right hand, but the goats on the left. Then shall the King say unto them on his right hand, Come, ye blessed of my Father, inherit the kingdom prepared for you from the foundation of the world:* Wow and wow! Jesus is speaking here of Judgment Day. The goats will be separated from the Sheep. The Sheep refer to His Elect, His Children. So, where are the goats today, those who died in the past, you ask? This place is called "Hades," which is not the final destination of the lost; Hell would be. But we see here that Jesus is separating the goats from the Sheep. Matthew 25:41 KJV *Then shall he say also unto them on the left hand, Depart from me, ye cursed, into everlasting fire, prepared for the devil and his angels:* Jesus sends those on

His left hand to everlasting fire, which is Hell, which was prepared for the fallen angels, the unclean spirits (demons), and Satan. Let me clear up any confusion about where and when The Bible says Christians go to Heaven. It's 2 Corinthians 5:8 KJV: *We are confident, I say, and willing rather to be absent from the body, and to be present with the Lord.* Here, Paul is referring to a Believer's death; he says that when a Christian dies, he or she is instantaneously with the Lord. Amen!

Let's get back to Jonah 3:1-4 KJV *And the word of the Lord came unto Jonah the second time, saying, Arise, go unto Nineveh, that great city, and preach unto it the preaching that I bid thee. So Jonah arose, and went unto Nineveh, according to the word of the Lord. Now Nineveh was an exceeding great city of three days' journey. And Jonah began to enter into the city a day's journey, and he cried, and said, "Yet forty days, and Nineveh shall be overthrown".* Jonah was spit out from the fish, and was given a second chance because of Jonah's prayers for his certain death. We see he reached Nineveh in a day because the fish brought him closer; God knew Jonah would pray that prayer. So, Jonah reaches Nineveh and **preaches only 8 words. I am sure he didn't try hard; he didn't preach with any love;** he preached with zero compassion, zero sympathy, zero empathy, and zero ambition, because he hated that mission, **hated the Ninevites.**

Let's see what happens next: it's Jonah 3:5-10 NKJV. *So the people of Nineveh believed God, proclaimed a fast, and put on sackcloth, from the greatest to the least of them. Then word came to the king of Nineveh; and he arose from his throne and laid aside his robe, covered himself with sackcloth and sat in ashes. And he caused it to be proclaimed and published throughout Nineveh by the decree of the king and his nobles, saying, Let neither man nor beast, herd nor flock, taste anything; do not let them eat, or drink water. But let man and beast be covered with sackcloth, and cry mightily to God;*

yes, let everyone turn from his evil way and from the violence that is in his hands. Who can tell if God will turn and relent, and turn away from His fierce anger, so that we may not perish? Then God saw their works, that they turned from their evil way; and God relented from the disaster that He had said He would bring upon them, and He did not do it.

The Ninevites took Jonah seriously, possibly because of the acid in the fish's stomach, which could have bleached his face, validating Jonah's experience, and possibly he was even spit out of the fish; the Bible is silent on that. **Or was it ALL God, who turned the hearts of the Ninevites to repent?** Jesus brings up this story Himself in Matthew 12:41 NLT: *"The people of Nineveh will stand up against this generation on judgment day and condemn it, for they repented of their sins at the preaching of Jonah. Now someone greater than Jonah is here, but you refuse to repent.* Here, Jesus speaks to the Pharisees and cites the story of Jonah. He says that those from Nineveh repented of their sins. They Were Counted for Righteousness (Saved), yet that was merely Jonah, and now in front of the Pharisees is the Son of God, who is Greater than Jonah by far, yet they would not believe. Back to Jonah 3:10, 4:1 NIV *When God saw what they did and how they turned from their evil ways, he relented and did not bring on them the destruction he had threatened. But to Jonah this seemed very wrong, and he became angry.*

God saved the Ninevites because they truly turned from their evil ways. We have to turn from our evil ways as well and focus on Jesus, follow Him, and all His Teachings. Jonah was upset because his plans did not prevail: to see the destruction of Nineveh. God and His Plans Did Prevail and Will Always Triumph. **This story shows us the greatest move of Salvation in the Bible.** Peter's first sermon at Pentecost, preaching to unbelievers, (3000) three thousand were converted in one day. **With Jonah using only 8 (eight) words, some say close to (500,000) Five Hundred Thousand were Saved.** I want to bring to your attention why I went to the book of Jonah: to show you that it's not always about love, love, love in preaching. No, it's not about using hundreds of words; it's ALL About God's Authority: Fearing God. Remember, **there was no fancy preaching, no foolish light show, no rock band, no smoke machine, no storytelling "pastor", no videos or cartoons** on a big screen, **no alter calls**, no used car salesman performances, no nonsense, just eight (8) words that put FEAR in the hearts of people who Were Moved. It's Jonah 3:4 NIV *Jonah began by going a day's journey into the city, proclaiming, "Forty more days and Nineveh will be overthrown."* **Has God planted enough FEAR into your heart that you repent?**

God, through His Sovereign Power, changed the Hearts of those hundreds of thousands in Nineveh; do you really think eight words from a bitter man would persuade a whole city? Try that today in the city of New York, San Francisco, or any city for that matter. **God's Will is past our understanding.** Did God save the Ninevites to show Jonah His Mercy and place it on full display, or to show us today **how far-reaching His Mercy, His Power, His Election, extends without any reason or any merit; oh, such Grace,** Grace and Grace! Let's jump back to Ephesians 2:8-9 KJV *For by grace are ye saved through faith; and **that not of yourselves**: it is the gift of God: Not of works, lest any man should boast.* Here, Paul is making it crystal clear, it's ALL Grace which is from God, and it's all Faith Which Is Given in Measure by GOD When One Is SAVED. **This is why a True Believer can never become an unbeliever because Faith Is A Gift From God!** That leaves Salvation being NOTHING from us and ALL from Him. The purpose here is that no one could boast, saying they were smarter and had chosen the right God; **no one could ever say they had anything to do with or contributed to their own Salvation.** Those who think different, thinking such power to claim salvation, to ask for it, beg for it, work for it, walking an aisle for it, say a prayer for it, thinking such Power from God is available at their beckon call, using their own will to achieve it, thinking salvation is within their grasp for the asking or taking; **such backwards thinking is only generated by the wicked, the false preacher, false teacher, and the lost.**

     The moral of The Book of Jonah is one of God's Doctrine of ELECTION. The whole Bible is about Jesus and Salvation through Election. Let's look a little closer; the storm listened to God, the big fish, the sailor, the captain, the people of Nineveh, and eventually God's own reluctant Prophet, Jonah. This proves **that man's own will can do nothing a**t all to prevent God's plans, nothing. **All of those Ninevites who repented were God's Chosen before the foundation of the world; their Names were all written in the Book of Life, which, as we now know, was written before the world was created.** God had a mission for Jonah; ask yourself, does God have a mission for you? When God wants us to move, talk, or listen **on His behalf, just do it.** Jonah's rebellion was only at his own peril, his own torment and anguish, and did nothing to prevent God's Will. Let's go to Romans 12:1-2 NKJV *I beseech you therefore, brethren, by the mercies of God, that you present your bodies a living sacrifice, holy, acceptable to God, which is your reasonable service. And do not be conformed to this world, but be transformed by the renewing of your mind, that you may prove what is that good and acceptable and perfect will of God.* A man or woman who is successful is one who finds out through God's Word what God wants him or her to accomplish with his or her life. It's never about money or houses, careers or fame. For me, it's writing books to feed His Sheep, giving out Bible tracts, and sharing the Gospel of John with those His Spirit within me prompts me to reach out to. **If you are one of His Children, God created you for His Glory, not yours.** It's Revelation 4:11 KJV *Thou art worthy, O Lord, to receive glory and honor and power: for thou hast created all things, and for thy pleasure they are and were created.* God created all things, for His Pleasure; are we living a life that is pleasing to God? Our bodies are on loan, our breath, our Spirit; our lives are God's for the taking. Ask yourself, ***"What have you done with what God has given to YOU?"***

Let's go to 1 Corinthians 6:19-20 KJV *What? know ye not that your body is the temple of the Holy Ghost which is in you, which ye have of God, and ye are not your own? For ye are bought with a price: therefore glorify God in your body, and in your spirit, which are God's.* This first Epistle of Paul to the Corinthians is, of course, addressed to Believers. Your Body is His Property, once Saved your Body Houses the Holy Spirit. The price Paul speaks of here is the life and resurrection of the Lord Jesus Christ. **His Death Paid the Full Price to Own YOU for His Purposes, His Use, You Belong 100% to Him.** We need to be a full expression of His Representation; an illustration of Heaven and not of this fallen world. We are His Ambassadors, and that includes being bold in His Truths. **Even if only using eight words** of warning, or eight words of the Gospel, <u>or eight words of Truth, which are infinitely better than saying or doing nothing in the face of one who needs Truth or Correction.</u> **God Will Honor Your Boldness**. **Your words will not return void!** Jump back to Isaiah 55:11 KJV *So shall my word be that goeth forth out of my mouth: it shall not return unto me* *void, but it **shall accomplish that which I please, and it shall prosper in the thing whereto I sent it.*** Yes, God's Word, when spoken to another, will do what God wants it to: either lead one to Salvation, soften a heart, or further harden a heart God wants hardened. Yet, as Charles Spurgeon said, ***"Just let the Lion out!"***

Martyn Lloyd Jones, a Protestant minister and medical doctor, was quoted as saying, ***"A Christian is the result of the operation of God, nothing less, nothing else. No man can make himself a Christian; God alone makes Christians...A Christian is one who has been created anew, and there is only one who can create, namely, God. It takes the power of God to make a Christian."*** Well said, Brother Martyn!

Chapter 10: Politics and "Religion?"

Many people say, ***"Don't speak about Politics or Religion."*** This is a subject that concerns ALL Believers and is so widely misunderstood. Why would Believers argue or debate either of these issues, which are clearly explained in God's Word? It's because few "Christians" read the Word of God in a way in which they should, by studying it; remember, it's like algebra! Let's begin to seek the answers, go to Romans 13:1-3 GNT *Let every soul be subject to the governing authorities. For there is no authority except from God, and the authorities that exist are appointed by God. Therefore whoever resists the authority resists the ordinance of God, and those who resist will bring judgment on themselves. For rulers are not a terror to good works, but to evil. Do you want to be unafraid of the authority? Do what is good, and you will have praise from the same.* Okay, now let's unpack these three verses. Let everyone obey their local police department, their government agencies, the federal government, and the President of their nation. **God placed those in power over you for a reason, His reasons.**

By resisting these powers, you bring upon yourself a penalty, possibly arrest, jail time, or worse. The law is not in place as a joke, but to uphold local, state, and federal laws. Paul goes on to explain that if you are obedient to such laws, there is nothing to worry about, and you will bring honor to your country in doing so. Let's jump back in the Word to Daniel 2:21 NIV *He changes times and seasons; he deposes kings and raises up others. He gives wisdom to the wise and knowledge to the discerning.* Daniel is a prophetic mouthpiece of God, and here Daniel is revealing God's power and shows the appointing of world leaders and who allows them to be in such a position to begin with. Jump over to Daniel 3:12-14 KJV *There are certain Jews whom thou hast set over the affairs of the province of Babylon, Shadrach, Meshach, and Abednego; these men, O king, have not regarded thee: they serve not thy gods, nor worship the golden image which thou hast set up. Then Nebuchadnezzar in his rage and fury commanded to bring Shadrach, Meshach, and Abednego. Then they brought these men before the king. Nebuchadnezzar spoke and said unto them, Is it true, O Shadrach, Meshach, and Abednego, do not ye serve my gods, nor worship the golden image which I have set up?* Let's unpack these three verses, here we see a refusal to listen to authority in fact these three men <u>Shadrach, Meshach, and Abednego worshipped</u> **The God of The Bible**; when they would not worship the golden image whom the King Nebuchadnezzar worshipped, these men were arrested and thrown in a fiery furnace; because of their defiance, but here we see an example of going against God's Word. For them, it worked out very, very well.

Because Jesus walked with them in the fire and the three were unharmed, and Nebuchadnezzar then told all his governors and people to worship the God of Shadrach, Meshach, and Abednego, and the King promoted them and caused them to prosper. This means when you do what God wants, sometimes things work out, and you change the minds of many. Just trust God and do what He wants you to. When you are told by your Governing agencies that the law states you can **kill a baby** once it's born! Or at any time one is in her mother's womb; both are against God's Word; don't do it, don't ever support it, don't condone it, and never vote for any party or platform that would agree with such murder into any office. **Don't vote wicked people (Liberals, Democrats, Socialists) into any held office in the land.** When you do, you are telling others you are **not a Christian**, and you too condone murder. <u>God's Word supersedes man's law. Sin, even if legalized by man, is still **sin** in the sight of God; His Doctrine is not ours to change!</u>

Christians vote for a party's PLATFORM that is closest to God's standards, and that is NEVER the Democratic platform! So many fake "believers" twist their whole thinking around and vote for an evil party, one that would murder babies; I ask you, seriously? Policymaking and laws that support God's Word are corroding in America as I write, yet we must vote for the lesser of the two evils, and yes, we must always vote! If you don't vote as a Christian, God would say to you, "**You reap what you sow**"; that's how we got to where we are today. Now, let's further explore this. Let's say your government says it's okay to allow gay marriages, again **don't support that**, rebuke those who do, and again teach God's Truths to all you can, instructing them never to vote anyone in any official office who buys into what God is against. It's not to say you hate them; you don't. They need Jesus and His Truths as we all do. You may say, "I am being harsh?" Well, this would only be the reaction from an unbeliever, not one who agrees with God's Written Word; again, I am writing to Believers.

God's Word will always supersede man's law, but be aware that God's moral laws are also for unbelievers as well. **The right thing to do is always the right thing;** for instance, killing, as in abortion, should not be considered, for ANY reason. Understand that she is housing another person, it's not her body; she would be killing her own child, and such is murder. The shedding of innocent blood is a term for the unjustified taking of human life in Matthew 19:17-18 NKJV. *So He said to him, "Why do you call Me good? No one is good but One, that is, God. But if you want to enter into life, keep the commandments." He said to Him, "Which ones?" Jesus said, "'You shall not murder,' 'You shall not commit adultery,' 'You shall not steal,' 'You shall not bear false witness.'* Here, Jesus answers the rich younger ruler's question about how to have eternal life. Note, Jesus starts with "You shall not Murder." **Those who think abortion is a mother's right fail to see life as God's privilege, which was not withheld from them.** The children who somehow escape abortion always grow up to speak out against it and never for it. There is a "morning after pill" available within 72 hours of a rape or of having sex and thinking you are pregnant, and you want to terminate that embryo, which is available over the counter in any drug store, rather than an abortion. The best protection is not a pill, or procedure, or abortion; it is **abstinence**, which means self-control, self-denial, **and not having sex before marriage. You should**

always choose adoption over abortion. Now that we as Christians realize that just understanding these two conditions of (abortion & gay marriage) and if these are supported by a "political party" or any politician, even one in any local agency, do not vote for them, **vote against them!** Do not vote anyone into any office who would agree with these ungodly polices or conditions or make excuses to justify them; such nonsense is from the evil one.

Their lack of morals and their secular mindset would rub off on their creation of certain rules and laws, which would also be against God's Word. This is how corruption enters our counties, cities, states, and federal governments: it starts with politics, and it starts with those who see these two sins (abortion & gay marriage) as okay. **Never buy into Satan's lie that one should not speak of politics and religion; those are the two most important subjects, which will build or destroy any nation.** Great nations fall because of their corrupt and evil-minded politicians who are bought with a price, who buy into the killing of babies in the womb. The world mocks those who follow Christ but loves a professing "Christian" who fits in with the world's agenda. This is not a true "Christian," but a make-believer, a counterfeit "Christian." Beware!

Therefore, you as a Christian must bring them both up to your friends, other so-called "Christians" (this will expose them as being fake), and all your family members. Look, **even if you lose all your friends and family for Truth's sake, is it worth it? Oh yes!** Think of what's eternal, not what's temporal. Matthew 10:34-37 NKJV *"Do not think that I came to bring peace on earth.* **I did not come to bring peace** *but a sword. For I have come to 'set a man against his father, a daughter against her mother, and a daughter-in-law against her mother-in-law'; and 'a man's enemies will be those of his own household.' He who loves father or mother more than Me is not worthy of Me. And he who loves son or daughter more than Me is not worthy of Me.* Jesus is teaching just how His coming to save the Few will affect the many. So many desire darkness over light, wanting wrong over what in God's Eyes is Right.

He came to divide, not to unite. He came to be the light, not to add to our darkness. He came to Teach Truth, not add to our error. He came to be The Salt, not the sugar. Through His Children (us), that we too should understand we must be the Light, the Salt, and the Truth. We must reveal and declare His Truths, even if we lose all we know in this world, but gain Him, and live for Him, for He Alone is Worthy! **Upholding God's Values and Beliefs in a fallen, corrupt, evil, liberal, and nasty world is not easy.** Just remember what Jesus said, and don't cast your Pearls before swine. But do your part and cast your vote, always vote; it's your duty, remember the morality and values of your nation are at risk and depend on your vote! In the days of old, God appointed Kings, and today He still does. **God uses His Children to vote for His people or those closest to His Values. We are responsible for being God's Mouthpiece and using our moral compass,** His Word, and the Holy Spirit as our guide. Remember, there is no such thing as a liberal "Christian" and no such thing as a "Christian/Democrat"; that's an oxymoron. You must be one or the other. **There are many "Christian" chameleons, which change their mindset** depending on who they are with and where they are. We call these pretenders **HYPOCRITES**. It's James 1:8 KJV: *A double minded man is unstable in all his ways.* Here, James (half-brother of Jesus) exposes the double-minded man and teaches that their minds are always changing and that they can't be trusted. Let's dig a little and look at Matthew 5:11 GNT: *"Happy are you when people insult you and persecute you and tell all kinds of evil lies against you because you are my followers."* Here, Jesus is Preaching from the Mount; He knows many of His Followers will be belittled, insulted, and ostracized by family, friends, and total strangers. It is because you now defend God's Word and not the worldly foolishness and lies, which you once did. Jesus says, *"Be Happy, Rejoice,* *because our Rewards Are Not of This World."* Be strong in God's Truths always; He is watching.

Don't be swayed by "FAKE NEWS". This is a short list of fake news liberal networks that aid and abet leftist lies. They refuse to cover real news; in fact, they omit it, and it goes unreported because it would expose their hidden agenda, revealing their deception, false representations, and spiteful intentions. **This short list includes CNN, CBS, PBS, NBC, ABC, NPR, and MSNBC (also known as MS NOW). Then there are countless leftist radio stations. These networks, along with others, serve as the mouthpieces for the Democratic Party, Satan.** Moreover, mainstream and global media are predominantly composed of **liberals loyal to a Satanic one-world system.** They do not genuinely believe in justice; instead, they support a "Just–Us" mentality that only benefits themselves, spewing lie after lie. Their payday will come someday; God will not be mocked— **woe to those who call good evil and evil good.** Don't be like the Pharisees and heathens who suggest you "love" God while thinking it's okay to vote against everything God stands against, such as killing babies, the homosexual lifestyle, the LGBTQIA+ agenda, and gay marriage. The leftist ideology is what Satan uses to promote his evil agenda. Labeling evil as personal freedoms, liberals are the worst of the worst. Yes, you can judge a book by its cover, the same way you judge a tree by its fruit. **Christians must apply the Bible to ALL areas of their life.** We should not assume that just being a Republican means one is saved; **no**, I am not saying that by virtue of a party's affiliation means God is in one's heart, but common sense is. **Moreover, we vote for the PLATFORM that best reflects God's Truths and His Standards and His Values, and in America, that is NEVER the Democratic platform!** People are going to love you or hate you. Don't waste time trying to control that. Spend your days pleasing God, not people. I want to hear God say, *"Well done, my good and faithful Servant."* How about you? I now watch real news on **Newsmax** and know what's really going on worldwide; I suggest you do the same!

134

Let's look at Luke 14:34-35 NIV: *Salt is good, but if it loses its saltiness, how can it be made salty again? It is fit neither for the soil nor for the manure pile; it is thrown out. "Whoever has ears to hear, let them hear"* Let's unpack these two verses the Salt supposed to be God's "Children" *but* if they don't do as The Bible instructs, if they don't do as Jesus Commands, if they agree in word but not in deed, saying they agree but vote against what God is for, or are affiliated with a party that condones abortion or gay marriage etcetera, they are **NOT truly God's Children**. Therefore, they are worthless to God and are thrown into Hell, where all false converts end up. When Jesus says, ***"Whoever has ears to hear, let them hear,"*** He is speaking to His Elect, because His Sheep hear His Voice and Obey. We looked at this verse before, but let's dig even deeper...John 10:26-30 KJV *But ye believe not, because ye are not of my sheep, as I said unto you.* **My sheep hear my voice,** *and I know them, and they follow me: And I give unto them eternal life; and they shall never perish, neither shall any man pluck them out of my hand. My Father, which gave them me, is greater than all; and no man is able to pluck them out of my Father's hand. I and my Father are one.*

Here, Jesus is distinguishing a fundamental difference between His Sheep and the goats. His Children Hear His Voice, Understand His Will, and Are Obedient to His Word. They are not the ones who only talk the talk, but those who walk the walk. Not those who only give lip service to God, but those who give up their lives to God. God is not asking us to clean up our lives; **He is Commanding Us to Lay Down Our Lives for Him,** which can only be established in His Power, not our own. There is never any guesswork or confusion about who elected whom or why. **God's Children are those who study His Word, heed His Commands, and Believe the Whole Bible, and don't try to find ways around God's Truths.** When a Child of God is wrong in an area, or their views on a subject or any matter are not in line with God's Word, they are easily corrected once God's Word is brought to their attention and explained. Thus, this book! **We must allow the Word of God to correct us, just as we**

allow it to reassure us! God Chose and provided His Children (Elect) for His Son, and in the previous verse, Jesus assures His Children that their Salvation and Eternity are Secure and protected in Him and in the Father. **A person who is hungry for God will seek His Presence every day, not just on Sundays!**

John Charles (J.C.) Ryle, an English Bishop in the 1800's, said, *"Let us seek friends that will stir us up about our prayers, our Bible reading, our use of time, our souls, and our salvation."* Well said, J. C. Ryle.

Undoubtedly, America is a Christian nation founded on Judeo-Christian principles and ideologies rooted in the Bible. Why should Christians pay attention to politics? Because God wants us to! Let's turn to **Jeremiah 29:7 NASB:** *"Seek the prosperity of the city where I have sent you into exile, and pray to the Lord on its behalf; for in its prosperity will be your prosperity."* We must do everything possible to **keep our nation as a whole God-fearing, family-oriented, and biblical**, since the well-being of our nation depends on the well-being of our states, cities, homes, and neighbors. Therefore, **we must reject liberalism. Every Christian has a civic duty to vote conservatively (Republican), period!**

Chapter 11: Some of the Most Misunderstood Bible Verses

Jeremiah 29:11 NIV *For I know the plans I have for you," declares the Lord, "plans to prosper you and not to harm you, plans to give you hope and a future.* Here is a verse that is misused and abused each day. So many take this verse and personalize it (put it on t-shirts), **this is how fake Christians live, with no concern, regard, or respect as to what God's Word Truly Means.** If you are in doubt about what a verse like this means, think about how God allowed His Chosen Apostles to live and die; **are you any better?** People think it means they may be going through tough times and use this verse as if God owes them something significant. Well, God does not owe us anything; we owe Him everything! Thinking this verse is about today's Believer would be misinterpreting God's Word to mean what you want it to mean, that's (Eisegesis). Which is used by false teachers and is not what God meant. To discern this verse correctly, one would be using (Exegesis).

The true meaning of this verse concerning this enormous promise is **God's promise to the nation of Israel for its future Salvation during the Tribulation. This verse has nothing at all to do with Christians today.** No one can simply "cherry pick" a verse and, on its face value, say its meaning is what it says (face value) without first applying hermeneutics to this or any verse, "who is it referring to," and when and why and what by **digging deeper than face value.** Don't be a "Christian" based on "face value" alone, but on heart, soul, body, and mind. **A mind saturated in God's Truths.** No one but a false teacher, or false believer, deceiver, or charlatan would want to make a verse mean what it does not mean. **Beware of such twisting.** Scripture is intended to be studied in light of the whole chapter, and to whom a verse is referring or directed, it's based on the totality of that chapter and, in some cases, the totality of the Whole Bible! **This is why "the verse of the day" mentality does not work. Christians should joyfully be digging deep into God's Holy Word Daily, using a Bible, NOT an "App."**

Matthew 7:7 NKJV *"Ask, and it will be given to you; seek, and you will find; knock, and it will be opened to you.* Here, Jesus is speaking to the crowds who need His Wisdom and His Mercy. Jesus meant things that are necessities, but more so things that were and are Spiritual; **remember, the Bible is a Spiritual Book.** He did not mean money, houses, or riches because throughout His Ministry, Jesus Only Served; He never gave riches to anyone, not homes, not buckets of gold, not horses, not silver. **He gave everlasting life, His Grace and Mercy to many.** He was not a genie in a bottle, but far more than that. He healed and raised the dead; He told some their sins were forgiven; He was, and is, God. **Nowhere in His New Testament did Jesus make anyone rich with gold or silver, but in and through Himself.** Jesus Himself is the Way, The Truth, and The Life. If you are His, your request **when you "knock" in Prayer is To Be More Like Him! More of Him and less of you.** He did say in Matthew 19:24 KJV *And again I say unto you, It is easier for a camel to go through the eye of a needle, than for a rich man to enter into the kingdom of God.* Jesus states that no one can be saved because of their wealth, and that, because of wealth, "Salvation" is not only difficult; Jesus said it would be easier to fit a camel through the eye of a sewing needle! **So many already serve a "god," and it's their money.** Jesus is expressing in a Comical Way, or is He Very Serious Here when He states how tough it is for a wealthy man to be a Christian?

1 Timothy 2:3-4 LSB *This is good and acceptable in the sight of God our Savior, who **desires** all men to be saved and to come to the full knowledge of the truth.;* let's unpack verse 3 and use verse 4 as well. We must distinguish between what God would like to see happen and what He actually does to make things happen, which **He WILLS to happen.** For us to distinguish between the two, we must consider all of Scripture, and that's not done by taking a verse out of context. Paul is writing to Timothy, who is facing challenging times teaching at the Church at Ephesus. **He is addressing and referring to Believers.** Paul is explaining God's Decree,

God's Eternal purpose **(which is NOT to save all men)**, meaning it's not His Will, not His Mandate. If it were, ALL men would be saved, and we know from scripture that is not true. All men do NOT come to the knowledge of Truth, because no one seeks after God, not one. As we know from studying Romans 3:10-11. Let's Dig Deeper...There are different aspects of God's Will. There is **His Sovereign Will,** which is unchangeable and will happen, i.e., God's Doctrine of Election. Remember, ALL things ultimately are in His Control; some things He MAKES happen by orchestrating countless events, and others He allows to happen, which will ultimately benefit His Elect. Romans 8:28 KJV *And we know that all things work together for good to them that love God, to them who are the called according to his purpose.* God's Moral Will gives us His clear Commands, which we should follow, but we don't. This is why Biblical consequences are certain. There is God's individual Will, which is His plan concerning each of our lives and determines our eternity. It will NOT fail. Not one of His Children will be lost. John 6:39 LSB *Now this is the will of Him who sent Me, that of all that He has given Me I lose nothing, but raise it up on the last day.* **God's Desire and His Will are two different things.** God does not want or desire people to sin, but we do! Jesus desires us to be perfect as His Father is, but we are NOT! Matthew 5:48 LSB *Therefore, you are to be perfect, as your heavenly Father is perfect.* There are other "wills" of God: His Determined (Sovereign) Will (which is revealed in His Word). This means ALL things are under His Control, and what God wants to happen will happen, without fail, as I noted. And, then there's **His Secret (Undetermined) Will;** His Will of His Good Pleasure, which can only be seen through a dark lens or not at all. **Yes, God would like to see all men repent of their sins and seek Jesus in His Word, because God hates sin.** But man does not seek His Son with full unvarnished commitment unless they are Born Again by God. **God's choices are determined by His Sovereign and Eternal Purpose and not His requests or desires.** Therefore, all things are determined by God's Sovereign Will and His

Commands. **All God wants us to know is contained in His Word, and we need to obey it.**

2 Peter 3:9 (KJV) *The Lord is not slack concerning his promise, as some men count slackness; but is longsuffering to us-ward, not willing that any should perish, but that all should come to repentance.* Let's unpack this verse as well. To understand this, we must again know **who Peter is addressing.** We must visit **2 Peter 1:1 (KJV)***: Simon Peter, a servant and an apostle of Jesus Christ, to them that have obtained **like precious faith** with us through the righteousness of God and our Savior Jesus Christ.* Okay, we now see Peter is **speaking to Believers**, not unbelievers. In verse 3:9, the Lord is not slacking concerning His promise (of Judgment Day), He will not allow any of His Children to perish (see Hell), but gives time for His Children to repent. **Are YOU repenting each day, seeking His Face?**

Revelation 3:20 NKJV *Behold, I stand at the door and knock. If anyone hears My voice and opens the door, I will come in to him and dine with him, and he with Me.* Here, Jesus is talking to a **wayward "church,"** a "church" at Laodicea, which is best known as part of the **group of false** "churches." **There is no answer, and Jesus never knocks!** If He wants a soul whom His Father has given to Him before the foundation of the world, **He will break down the door!** Remember, Jesus <u>knocked</u> Paul off his horse when He wanted his attention. We see how that all turned out.

Philippians 4:13 AMP *I can do all things [which He has called me to do] through Him who strengthens and empowers me [to fulfill His purpose—I am self-sufficient in Christ's sufficiency; I am ready for anything and equal to anything through Him who infuses me with inner strength and confident peace.]* I used this version in The Amplified Bible because it's much more revealing here to what this Truth is. A Christian can do all things God calls him to do, with God's help, absolutely! It's not about dunking a basketball or making a touchdown. **It's about Him, JESUS, and what you do to glorify Him and His Father, who are One.** IT'S NOT ABOUT YOU! In The Will of God, you can do all things, but on your own, you can do nothing. <u>God empowers you to glorify Him, not yourself.</u>

Psalms 37:4 KJV *Delight thyself also in the Lord: and he shall give thee the desires of thine heart.* I have seen this one on bumper stickers and t-shirts; also used by many false teachers' "pastors" who attempt to coerce "church" goers to walk an aisle and ask Jesus into their hearts so that He can grant their wishes. The Truth is that a Christian's desires will all be reoriented once Born Again; **such desires (If YOU are HIS) are all towards Christ, more of Him and less of YOU!** To be delighted in the Lord is to **die to oneself** and be ALL in for God. **Our Desires Should Always Be God's Desires for Us,** <u>which are to be fully committed to Him and live and do things **His Way, not ours** and definitely not the world's.</u> **To determine what delights God is to study His Word, Obey it! Spread the Gospel, plant seeds of Truth; contribute in some way to help many others see why they, too, need Jesus.**

Romans 8:28 KJV *And we know that all things work together for good to them that love God, to them who are the called according to his purpose.* Here we have yet another Election verse. Let's look at this closely, we (Christians) know all things (everything) works together for good (we don't always see it) to (Christians) those Called (His Elect) for God's Purpose, again **God's Purpose, His Pleasure, not ours.**

I think about the Apostle Paul's life, and these four verses come to mind. Let's dig in at 2 Corinthians 11:24-28 TLB. *Five different times the Jews gave me their terrible thirty-nine lashes. Three times I was beaten with rods. Once I was stoned. Three times I was shipwrecked. Once I was in the open sea all night and the whole next day. I have traveled many weary miles and have been often in great danger from flooded rivers and from robbers and from my own people, the Jews, as well as from the hands of the Gentiles. I have faced grave dangers from mobs in the cities and from death in the deserts and in the stormy seas and from men who claim to be brothers in Christ but are not. I have lived with weariness and pain and sleepless nights. Often I have been hungry and*

thirsty and have gone without food; often I have shivered with cold, without enough clothing to keep me warm. Then, besides all this, I have the constant worry of how the churches are getting along:
As we all can see, things here do not appear to be working out for Paul at all, yet here we are. We are wiser and see into the lives of those who turned this world upside down to bring us The Truth of God's Word and to spread The Gospel. **This is the good of all of Paul's suffering, according to God's Purpose, not mine or yours.** God knew all of Paul's afflictions; He knew Paul's troubles beforehand and **used them to build him into an unshakable pillar for Jesus Christ,** and God can do the same for you. (Why so few takers?) The "working together for good" is in Heaven; or towards what would be eternal, **sometimes you get a glimpse of God moving on this side of Heaven, most times we don't,** but when you do, count it all joy!

Some useful observations:

1 Corinthians 13:8 KJV ***Charity*** *never faileth: but whether there be prophecies, they shall fail; whether there be tongues, they* ***shall cease****; whether there be knowledge, it shall vanish away.* I use this verse when I choose a commentary, if the writer does not have the courage to say "tongues" have ceased. I place that commentary back on the shelf. There is also something significant about Bible translations (versions). Check out the following observation.

1 Corinthians 13:4 KJV *Charity suffereth long, and is kind; charity envieth not; charity vaunteth not itself, is not puffed up.* The closest true Greek and Hebrew version of The Bible is the King James Version. Let me prove it here; other versions lack clarity and a precise definition of the accurate translation of Greek and Hebrew. Notice in the above verse, the word CHARITY charity is not the same as "love," which all the other versions of the Bible buy into. Love is an overused word; love is a two-way street with most. You love me, so I love you too, kind of thing. I love my cat, dog, or my ice cream sandwich. **But Charity is way different; it's a**

one-way street! Have you ever given something to someone and expected nothing back in return? Have you ever given money to a homeless man? Did you get a receipt? **Have you ever helped someone you knew could never repay you? That's Charity.**

Thus, the word Charity, **God's Love is Charity**, Charity towards His Children, which is 100% unmerited, undeserved Charity. We, the Elect, could **never** pay Him back. This is one reason why God's Children joyfully tell others of Jesus through The Gospel. Give our testimonies to others, sharing the awesome joy Salvation brings. We hope and pray to Father God, through Jesus our Savior, that our families and loved ones come to know Him and be saved. We pray for those we know or have just met to come to know Jesus and be saved. I beg Jesus to open the eyes of those reading this book, to grow in Him, and if they are not saved, to be saved by GOD.

If anything, you read from this book or any of God's Words so moved your heart as to want to know Him more; if your eyes and ears are newly opened through the writings in the book, **the Bible Verses in this book.** That means God is working on you and your heart; Rejoice! May He use even this mere book as a tool or an instrument to open your eyes to Him. I pray that...for He is ABLE. That is my prayer for each reader. If you have no burden for the souls of others, I would doubt your Salvation. Do you feel deep compassion for the lost? **You should speak up, stand up, and not back down when confronted with the evil issues each day brings. Be an outspoken Ambassador for Christ! He Alone is Worthy! Amen and Amen!**

Since first publishing this book in 2020, I have authored several other works. You can find books and short videos on the website, and books are also available for purchase.

www.JosephMalara.com

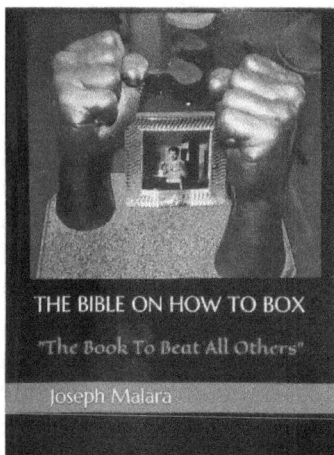
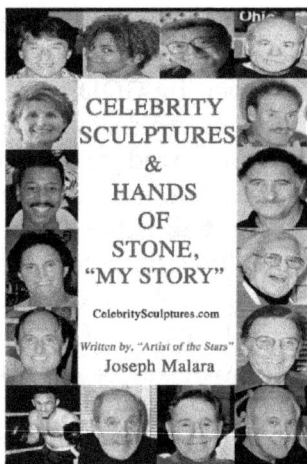

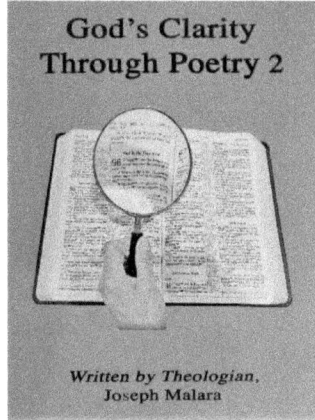

God's Clarity through Poetry

God's Clarity Through Poetry 2

Written by Theologian, Joseph Malara

Digging Deeper into God's Truth Defines a "Christian"

LOVE THEM ENOUGH TO TELL THEM THE TRUTH,

HOW THEY HANDLE IT IS BETWEEN THEM & GOD!

Over 390 Bible Verses Used & Explained!
11 Intriguing Chapters of Controversey
Regarding God's Truth EXPOSED...
How Can The Truth Change *Your* Life?

Written by Theologian, Joseph Malara

The Guide to Christian Dating, Marriage and Sex

Joseph Malara
JosephMalara.com

www.JosephMalara.com

WWW.JOSEPHMALARA.COM

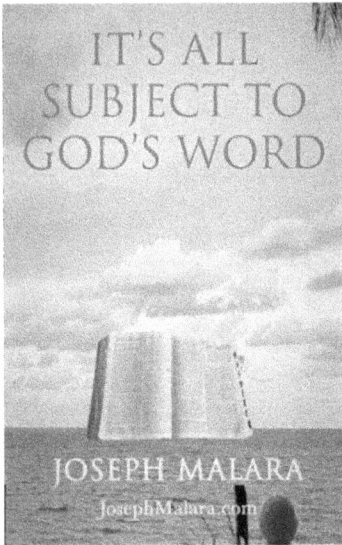

www.ingramcontent.com/pod-product-compliance
Lightning Source LLC
Chambersburg PA
CBHW072019040426
42447CB00009B/1664